AUG 10 '04

D0069718

COVERING THE INTIFADA

How the Media Reported the Palestinian Uprising

By Joshua Muravchik

THE WASHINGTON INSTITUTE FOR NEAR EAST POLICY

All rights reserved. Printed in the United States of America. No part of this publication may be reproduced or transmitted in any form or by any means, electronic or mechanical, including photocopy, recording, or any information storage and retrieval system, without permission in writing from the publisher.

© 2003 by The Washington Institute for Near East Policy

Published in 2003 in the United States of America by The Washington Institute for Near East Policy, 1828 L Street NW, Suite 1050, Washington, DC 20036.

Library of Congress Cataloging-in-Publication Data

Muravchik, Joshua.
Covering the intifada: how the media reported the Palestinian uprising / Joshua Muravchik.
     p. cm.
ISBN 0-944029-85-X
1. Al-Aqsa Intifada, 2000– —Press coverage—United States. 2. Israel—Politics and government—20th century—In mass media. 3. Journalism—Objectivity—United States. I. Title.

DS119.765.M87 2003
070.4'49956053—dc21

                                          2003012382

Front/back cover photo of press photographers and cameramen near the Church of the Nativity in Bethlehem, April 8, 2002; Israeli soldiers (unseen) fire smoke grenades in background © AP Wide World Photos. Back cover photo of author courtesy of American Enterprise Institute. Cover design by Alicia Gansz.

The Author

Joshua Muravchik is a resident scholar at the American Enterprise Institute and an adjunct scholar of The Washington Institute for Near East Policy. He is the author of six previous books (most recently, *Heaven on Earth: The Rise and Fall of Socialism* [Encounter Books, 2002]) and hundreds of articles. His op-ed pieces have appeared in all major U.S. dailies, his longer articles in *New York Times Magazine, Foreign Affairs, Foreign Policy, Commentary, New Republic, Weekly Standard,* and numerous other journals. His previous studies of the news media include one book (*News Coverage of the Sandinista Revolution* [American Enterprise Institute, 1988]) and a handful of major articles, among them "Misreporting Lebanon," published in *Policy Review* in 1983. He holds a bachelor's degree from the City College of New York and a doctorate in international relations from Georgetown University.

• • •

The opinions expressed in this monograph are those of the author and not necessarily those of The Washington Institute for Near East Policy, its Board of Trustees, or its Board of Advisors.

THE WASHINGTON INSTITUTE
for Near East Policy

*An educational foundation supporting scholarly research
and informed debate on U.S. interests in the Near East*

Executive Committee

Chairman
Michael Stein

Vice Presidents
James Schreiber
SENIOR VICE PRESIDENT
Charles Adler
Benjamin Breslauer
Robert Goldman
Walter P. Stern

President
Fred S. Lafer

Secretary
Richard S. Abramson

Treasurer
Martin J. Gross

Emeritus Members
Maurice Deane
Leonard Goodman

*Founding President/
Chairman Emerita*
Barbi Weinberg

Committee Members
Howard Berkowitz
Richard Borow
Gerald Friedman
Roger Hertog
Bernard Leventhal
Fred Schwartz
Merryl Tisch

Board of Advisors

Warren Christopher
Lawrence S. Eagleburger
Alexander Haig
Max M. Kampelman
Jeane Kirkpatrick

Samuel W. Lewis
Edward Luttwak
Michael Mandelbaum
Robert C. McFarlane
Martin Peretz
Richard Perle

James Roche*
George P. Shultz
Paul Wolfowitz*
R. James Woolsey
Mortimer Zuckerman

* *resigned upon entry to government service, 2001*

Institute Staff

*Director of Policy and
Strategic Planning*
Robert Satloff

*Counselor, Turkish Research
Program*
Mark Parris

*Coordinator, Turkish Research
Program/Soref Fellow*
Soner Cagaptay

2003 Visiting Fellows
Maj. Gen. (ret.) Jacob
  Amidror (IDF), IRA
  WEINER FELLOW
Jinying Fang
Martin Kramer, WEXLER-
  FROMER FELLOW
Hazem Saghie

2003 Visiting Military Fellows
Michael Knights
  MENDELOW DEFENSE
  FELLOW
Lt. Col. Eric Mathewson
  UNITED STATES AIR FORCE
Lt. Col. Yoram Yoffee
  ISRAEL DEFENSE FORCES

*Director/Ziegler
Distinguished Fellow*
Dennis Ross

Director of Development
Laura Milstein

Development Associate
Marilyn Turner

Chief Financial Officer
Laura Hannah

Controller
Robin Edwards

Executive Assistant
Marguerite Dale

Administrator
Nina Bisgyer

Events Coordinator
Rebecca Saxton

Administrative Assistant
Kim Baker

Director of Publications
Alicia Gansz

Editorial Associate
George Lopez

Editorial Assistant
Veronica Kim

Deputy Director
Patrick Clawson

Senior Fellows
Michael Eisenstadt
Matthew Levitt
David Makovsky

2003 Soref Fellows
Max Abrahms
Avi Jorisch
Jonathan Schanzer

Associates
Simon Henderson
Ze'ev Schiff
Jeffrey White
Ehud Ya'ari

Adjunct Scholars
Hirsh Goodman
Joshua Muravchik
Daniel Pipes
Michael Rubin
Harvey Sicherman
Raymond Tanter

Table of Contents

Preface

For the thousand days since September 2000, Israelis and Palestinians have been at war. Unlike
a conventional conflict, this war began with
Molotov cocktails and police batons, moved to
deadly suicide bombings and tank-backed retaliatory raids, and then was characterized by the
firing of homemade mortars and "targeted kill-
ings" by helicopter gunships. So far, about 3,000
have died, with thousands more wounded. Although
popularly known as the "Palestinian uprising"—or
intifada—these events should more accurately be
regarded as war.

Popular perception, however, is often what matters most in the world of international politics,
and this is certainly true of the Israeli-Palestinian conflict. Perhaps no international dispute
has been the subject of as much press coverage—
television, radio, print, and web-based—as the
battle over rights, land, security, and survival
in the Holy Land. Reportage from Ramallah, Gaza,
Jerusalem, and Tel Aviv often sets the diplomatic
agenda; grisly images of human carnage at pizze-
rias, cafes, outdoor markets, and refugee camps
often frame the debates in the White House, the
United Nations Security Council, and capitals
around the world. In the Middle East, journalists
are often more than just conveyors of news—they
have the power to shape the news and, in so doing, determine the path of future events.

Despite the significant role that journalists
play as actors in this conflict, they are rarely
the subject of rigorous, methodical, academic
investigation. Two years ago, The Washington Institute decided to address this lacuna by
undertaking a major research project to assess
the quality and accuracy of reportage on the
Palestinian "uprising" by elite U.S. media.

Thanks to a generous grant from Janine and Peter Lowy, valued Institute trustees, we were able to commission noted scholar and historian Joshua Muravchik to undertake this effort. Given Dr. Muravchik's previous work on media coverage—he is author of the definitive work on reportage of the Israeli invasion of Lebanon, a book on news coverage of the Nicaraguan revolution, and numerous articles on how the media has covered issues ranging from U.S. defense spending to Cold War clashes with the Soviet Union—we were delighted that he agreed to take on this project. After two years of research, including reviewing dozens of hours of videotape and thousands of column inches of newspaper reportage, we are proud to present this study.

After dissecting ten newsworthy episodes during the course of the uprising, Dr. Muravchik presents an innovative way to evaluate the professionalism of U.S. reporters, producers, editors, and television anchors. His findings include the good, the bad, and the ugly: outstanding reportage by some, misinformed and error-plagued reportage by others, and patterns of outrageous reportage by a select few. Bias, he argues, is certainly present but not rampant. Superficiality; misinformation; lack of historical context; and reliance on narrow, skewed, or unrepresentative sources are greater and more pervasive problems. Although much of the reportage he evaluates is flawed, the problems, he notes optimistically, can be fixed—but only if journalists are willing to address them honestly, directly, and with an open mind. Perhaps most usefully, Dr. Muravchik offers a set of suggestions for improving the quality, depth, and accuracy of the reportage—suggestions that should reach the desks of top executives at major news outlets throughout the United States.

We believe a study on media reportage of the Arab-Israeli conflict is long overdue. This is a first installment of what we expect to be a regular feature on our research agenda.

Michael Stein
Chairman

Fred S. Lafer
President

introduction

The appalling violence between Israelis and Palestinians that began in September 2000 has been one of the most painful episodes in the history of the modern Middle East. People on both sides, and many outsiders, had hoped that the famous handshakes on the White House lawn in 1993 that sealed the Oslo agreements marked the beginning of the end of the Arab-Israeli conflict. Now those hopes seemed to have turned to ashes.

For Israel, the pain of dashed hopes was compounded by the sense that much of the world blamed it for the breakdown and looked upon the Palestinians as the victims. Some Israelis accused the international news media of bias against Israel. On the other side, however, some Arabs insisted it was they who were the victims of unfair coverage. Noting that they were criticized from both directions, news organizations tended to read this as proof of their objectivity, a plausible inference that was not necessarily well founded.

To assess the coverage, I have undertaken this study on behalf of The Washington Institute for Near East Policy. It has been designed in collaboration with the Institute's director, Robert Satloff. It examines seven national news outlets: the *New York Times,* the *Washington Post,* and five television networks (ABC, CBS, NBC, CNN, and Fox). The television coverage examined is limited to the main nightly news broadcasts, which are a fixed ritual on the three older networks. Neither CNN nor Fox has an evening news program exactly equivalent to those of the older networks, but I have done my best to select the closest analogue.

Because it was beyond my ability to study two years of news reports, Dr. Satloff and I selected ten critical moments in the unfolding of this conflict, or the "al-Aqsa intifada," as it is sometimes called. For each of these, I have studied the news reports over a five-day period, generally beginning two days before some highlight

event occurred and continuing until two days afterward. We make no claim that these were the ten
most important moments, since such a determination would have no particular relevance to the
purposes of this study. Our goal was merely to
take a manageable slice of these two years for
examination. We might have taken fifty days at
random, except that we wanted to make sure to
choose days on which the Middle East tragedy was
indeed in the news. (The *Times* and the *Post* carried at least one story from the area almost
daily, but the television news often carried nothing
about it except on those days when the conflict
had heated up.)

To avoid inadvertent prejudice resulting from
our selection of events, we tried to select a mix
of occasions, including some on which the main
story was about diplomacy and others on which it
was about violence; some on which most of the
victims were Israeli and others on which most
were Palestinian. Our chosen episodes are "front
loaded," that is, weighted toward the earlier part
of the conflict. This is in part because there was
so much drama at the outset, in part because the
early reportage set a tone for much that followed, and in part because this study has taken
some time to produce (being originally designed
earlier in the intifada).

For the fifty selected days, I read care-
fully all news stories relevant to the Arab-
Israeli conflict that appeared in the two
newspapers. To examine the television coverage,
I viewed each broadcast (thanks to the facilities of the Television News Archive of Vanderbilt
University) and, in addition, read transcripts
of the broadcasts.

Beyond the care I tried to take in examining
the material, this study has no formal methodol-
ogy. I find quantitative media analysis almost
invariably unpersuasive. The number of times that
a given term or thought appears in news reports is
easy to count, but what does it prove? My "meth-

odology" is common sense. I am aiming to assess accuracy, fairness, and balance. These are values that lie at the heart of the American practice of journalism. My goal is to judge whether the news organizations met these standards, and, if they failed, then to assess how often and how severely. If only one or two of a journalist's many stories fall short, not much should be made of it; no one is perfect (not even media critics). Yet, if a journalist or news organization repeatedly fails in the realms of accuracy or fairness, this amounts to a serious lapse of professionalism.

Where I have spotted a story that I believe merits criticism, I cite it and explain what I think is wrong. In most cases, I refrain from commenting on editorials, columns, or explicit opinion pieces, even though I have read many opinions with which I disagree. My concern in this study is not to counter such opinions but to judge whether the newspapers and networks I have examined have met the highest standards of their profession. In a few cases, however, I have noted erroneous assertions of fact within editorials, and in one case what seemed to me an absurd supposition.

Much more often, I criticize editorializing within news stories, that is, reportage that seems strongly colored by the journalist's opinions. In addition, as I shall explain more in the body and the conclusion of the study, I believe I uncovered some systemic problems endemic to the asymmetry of the Israeli-Palestinian conflict that have derogated from the quality of the coverage of these tragic events.

One obvious flaw in my method is the familiar "dog that did not bark" problem. Just as news organizations are often criticized for not reporting good news, so my analysis focuses on instances of dereliction on the part of journalists rather than on the many informative stories in which I found nothing to fault. Like others who

study political events, I rely heavily on the
accounts of reporters from whose knowledge and
skill I benefit. That they often have to work in
hazardous conditions makes me all the more in-
debted to them.

Lastly, I must address the question of my own
standing to judge. I do not claim to come to this
subject as a dispassionate neutral. I am a Jew and
a supporter of Israel. By the last term I mean
that I strongly uphold Israel's right to exist
(which I believe is a central question of the
Arab-Israeli conflict), not that I necessarily
agree with every action of each Israeli government. I do not consider that disagreement with,
or criticism of, Israeli policy is tantamount to
being "anti-Israel." Israelis themselves are often raucous in their own political disputes. Yet,
obsessive or one-sided criticism of Israeli policies may reflect a deeper animosity to the state.

I do not believe that my strong support for
Israel's existence prevents me from producing a
rigorous analysis. As individuals and citizens,
news reporters have opinions and political alle-
giances, yet this does not make it impossible for
them to meet standards of accuracy and fairness.
Likewise, I have made every effort not to be
overmastered by my predilections, but rather to
carry out this study with a discipline of reason,
objectivity, fairness, and, of course, fidelity
to fact. Readers will judge my success or failure
at meeting those standards.

episode 1:

Sharon Visits
the Temple Mount

The "al-Aqsa intifada"
began on September 28,
2000, following the vis-
it by Ariel Sharon, then the leader of Israel's
parliamentary opposition, to the Temple Mount.
Sharon's stated purpose was to underscore his
opposition to relinquishing Israel's sovereignty
over Judaism's holiest site, an issue that had
been on the table at the Camp David summit two
months before. This position is anathema to the
Palestinians, who also want sovereignty over
the same place, which they call al-Haram al-
Sharif—the location of Jerusalem's most sacred
Muslim shrine and one of Islam's earliest ob-
jects of devotion, the al-Aqsa mosque. Sharon,
moreover, is a particularly offensive figure to
them because of his share of responsibility for
the 1982 slaughter of hundreds of Palestinians
by Lebanese Christian militiamen in the Beirut
refugee camps of Sabra and Shatilla.

The riot that followed hard on the heels of
Sharon's visit to the mount ended without loss
of life, although dozens of rioters and Israeli
policemen were injured. The next day, rioting
recommenced, spreading throughout the territories and resulting in several deaths. In the
original Palestinian version of events, Sharon's
visit was a provocation that inevitably sparked
a spontaneous expression of rage from the grass
roots. To the Israelis, the rioting was either
orchestrated or encouraged by Palestinian officials in order to strengthen their bargaining
position.

It is hard to doubt that the Palestinians found
Sharon's visit provocative, but the renewed riot-
ing on a second day, and then a third and fourth,
suggested that additional factors were at work.
This was confirmed some months later by Marwan
Barghouti, probably the most important leader of
the intifada, in an interview with the *New Yorker*.
"The explosion would have happened anyway,"
Barghouti stated. "It was necessary in order to

9

protect Palestinian rights. But Sharon provided a good excuse. He is a hated man."[1]

News organizations varied in the amount of emphasis given to Sharon's visit. The *New York Times,* which almost invariably characterized Sharon as "right-wing" or "rightist" (although the paper rarely, if ever, referred to the Labor Party prime minister, Ehud Barak, as "left-wing" or "left-ist"), focused more intently than any other out-let on Sharon's role in stimulating the violence.

The first day's riots were described by *Times* correspondent Deborah Sontag as "clashes . . . provoked by Mr. Sharon's visit" (September 29, 2000), which was fair enough. The next day, how-ever, a *Times* editorial underscored the point, chastising Sharon for having behaved "provoca-tively" and explaining to readers that "authority over [the Temple Mount] is the most sensitive remaining issue in the peace talks . . . the key to a final settlement." This was simply wrong: sovereignty over the Temple Mount was one of a handful of crucial issues that remained unre-solved, including borders and the so-called "right of return" of Arabs who had fled Israel in 1948, arguably the most sensitive issue of all. That evening, NBC's Tom Aspell, perhaps having read the *Times*' take, made the same mistake, commenting that "the whole Middle East peace process is dead-locked over which side will control" the mount.

On October 1, the *Times* was still focused on Sharon's pilgrimage, as correspondent William Orme wrote of "the third day of fierce fighting set off by the defiant visit." And two days after that, Orme wrote much the same again: "A defiant visit by Israel's right-wing opposition leader to the most sacred Islamic site in Jerusalem ignited Palestinian protests." In this recapitulation, Orme reminded his readers of the importance of the mount to Muslims but failed to mention its (still more primary) importance to Jews, although he might just as easily have used a phrase such as "a site sacred to both faiths." By stating the one

fact without the other, Orme risked leaving the
impression that Sharon's aim was to set foot gratuitously on a Muslim shrine when in fact it was
to assert Israel's claim to a Jewish shrine. Even
if his action was ill timed or ill considered,
there is a considerable difference between the
two intentions.

This points to an additional issue, namely,
that the site is holy to Christians as well, but
no mention of this fact was found in the coverage
examined for this study. It was as if the inten-
sity of the Jewish-Muslim tug-of-war canceled out
Christian interests entirely.

On October 3, another *Times* editorial summed up
the events this way: "The precipitating incident
was a provocative and irresponsible visit by the
Likud leader, Ariel Sharon. . . . But the fighting
has now taken on a life of its own." In other
words, the culprits were (1) Sharon and (2) the
impersonal force of momentum. This interpretation
was striking for what it omitted. The day after
Sharon's visit—the day that the violence turned
deadly—was a Friday, and an estimated 22,000 worshipers packed al-Aqsa for weekly services. They
were treated to a vitriolic and incendiary sermon
by the imam, Shaykh Hayan al-Idrisi, known for
his outspoken anti-Semitism and opposition to the
Camp David negotiations, who warned that "the Jews"
were intending to replace the mosque with a synagogue or temple. He added hortatively, "The Muslims are ready to sacrifice their lives and blood
to protect the Islamic nature of Jerusalem and El
Aksa!"[2]

In her account of that day's violence, the
Times' Sontag made brief mention of the sermon
in the twenty-sixth paragraph of a twenty-seven-
paragraph story, citing Israeli police officials
who pointed to it as an incitement. Her account
agreed that the sermon "did . . . raise anxieties
by talking about Jewish extremists," but this was
a misleading description since the sermon was
squarely aimed at "the Jews" per se, not at "ex-

tremists." A few days later, *Washington Post* correspondent Lee Hockstader gave something of the
sermon's flavor, quoting the shaykh as having
encouraged worshipers to "eradicate the Jews from
Palestine" (October 4).

None of the television news broadcasts examined in this study carried any mention of the
sermon. Nor did any explore the larger question
to which it pointed about the role of the Palestinian leadership in instigating the violence.
The *Post*'s Hockstader reported that, beginning on
the third day of violence, Palestinian television
"carried archival footage [of] the Palestinian
uprising of the late 1980s and early 90s, and
played militant songs urging Palestinians to rise
up and take to the streets" (October 4). This was
not reported in the *Times* or on any of the television networks, according to the findings of
this study. Neither did any of the networks report the fact that the Palestinian Authority (PA)
closed schools during the first several days of
the intifada, apparently to encourage students to
take part in the riots. (PA minister of information Yasir Abed Rabbo denied that this was the
motive, arguing that the schools were closed to
protect the children from Israeli snipers.[3] But
this explanation is unpersuasive since the school
closures were part of an official Palestinian
"general strike" and since those youngsters who
were hit by Israeli gunfire were almost always
involved in rock throwing or standing nearby and
rarely if ever were just walking to school.)

In one rare case in which the question of
Palestinian incitement was raised on U.S. television, it was with a sarcastic twist that empha-
sized Israeli culpability. On the fourth day of
rioting, ABC correspondent Gillian Findlay reported that "Sharon . . . whose visit to the site
of their sacred mosque sparked these riots . . .
refused to accept responsibility" (October 1).
Then she added, referring to the Barak government, "The men who could have stopped Sharon's

visit and didn't today blamed Palestinian leaders." In other words, Israeli complaints about
Palestinian incitement were not reported
straight—as Palestinian complaints about Israeli
behavior often were on ABC—but rather in a way
that made the Israeli complaint itself a dam-
nable hypocrisy.

The second day of violence, which happened to
be the Jewish New Year, began when worshipers
emerged from al-Aqsa, where they had heard Shaykh
al-Idrisi's sermon. Hurling thousands of rocks
and bottles, they besieged an Israeli police post
nearby and began raining projectiles on Jews praying
below at the Wailing Wall, which is located at the
base of the mount. Israeli police escorted Jewish
worshipers away from the wall and then charged up
onto the mount in order to rescue their comrades
in the besieged outpost. Firing rubber-coated bullets and sometimes, it seems, live ammunition,
they caused the death of four Palestinians. An
Israeli soldier died in nearby Qalqilya that day
when his Palestinian counterpart in a joint patrol turned on him suddenly and gunned him down
along with another Israeli who survived his wounds.

The *Times'* account of that day's grim events
clearly reported the stoning of Jewish worshipers
at the Wailing Wall (Orme, October 1), but the
Post's story failed to mention it. Of the three
television networks reporting the events on that
evening's news, CBS gave the clearest account,
with reporter David Hawkins explaining that "the
Israelis opened fire after Palestinian protesters
showered rocks and bottles down on Jewish worshipers and tourists" (September 29). NBC's version was much less informative. "Israeli riot police
stormed the shrine, opening fire with rubber bullets and live ammunition on Palestinians who were
throwing stones," reported Tom Brokaw, without
mentioning the Wailing Wall or the police outpost
(September 29). Then he added that "the riots
began after Israel's conservative Ariel Sharon
went to the Temple Mount to show that Jews were in

control." There was no way for viewers to know
that Sharon's visit had occurred the day before,
nor about the connection between the riots and
that day's services at al-Aqsa.

The most remarkable reportage was on ABC, where
Gillian Findlay described the violence on the
mount without mentioning the assault on the worshipers at the Wailing Wall or the siege of the
police outpost. Indeed, her choice of words seemed
to downplay any Palestinian provocation: "Israeli
police and soldiers rarely come here. This is the
second day in a row they have flexed their muscles
here, and Palestinians are furious," she stated
(September 29). This one-sided version followed
an opening by anchor Peter Jennings in which he
declared that "four Palestinians were killed by
Israelis on [the Temple Mount] today." No mention
was made of the Israeli who was killed by a Palestinian in Qalqilya.

Findlay went on for several sentences blaming
Sharon for the outbreak, citing both Palestinian
and Israeli critics of his visit the previous day
and concluding thus: "Sharon said he came to insist that Israel must control this place. Palestinians again today vowed that would never happen."
This conclusion, perhaps a pale echo of the shaykh's
incendiary warnings, suggested that Sharon was
out to change the status quo. In truth, Sharon's
gesture was aimed at reaffirming the status quo
that had existed since 1967, under which Israel
claimed sovereignty over the mount but left its
administration in the hands of the Muslim clergy.
This had been put in question by Prime Minister
Barak's willingness at Camp David to relinquish
Israel's sovereignty.

Findlay also reported, without any show of
doubt or opportunity for denial from the other
side, that "doctors who treated the wounded accused the soldiers of aiming to kill." Since
Jennings had stated that, in addition to the four
dead, 200 Palestinians had been injured, this
claim by Palestinian medical personnel was all

but absurd on its face. If less than 2 percent of the injured died, what was the likelihood that the Israelis were "aiming to kill"? And how could the doctors tell this from the wounds? What could they deduce from the wounds of the 98 percent who survived? None of the other networks saw fit to air the "aiming to kill" accusation.

The third day's clashes were still more violent, with a larger number of deaths, highlighted by that of twelve-year-old Mohammed al-Dura, whose last terrible hour was caught on film by a Palestinian cameraman for a French television network. Mohammed and his father cowered behind a concrete barrel at the Netzarim junction in Gaza, where Palestinian rioters had besieged an Israeli military outpost. The rioters hurled rocks and Molotov cocktails, and some of them fired guns. From their fortified position, Israeli soldiers responded with gunfire. The boy was hit, and his father appealed in vain for a halt to the firing. A half hour or so later, the son was hit again and died beside his father, who himself suffered nine separate bullet wounds but survived. Young al-Dura at once became "a potent new symbol of what angry Palestinians contend is their continued victimization" (*New York Times,* Orme, October 2). ABC's Findlay reported that "the video of twelve-year-old Mohammed plays on Palestinian television nonstop." Then she added, with apparent indignation, "It has appeared on Israel's most popular TV station exactly twice," implying that this amounted to downplaying the story.

Initially, most U.S. news organizations were cautious about saying who had fired the fatal shots, noting only that the boy had died "in a crossfire" (CBS, October 1). The one on-scene correspondent from the news organizations covered in this study who immediately blamed Mohammed's death on "Israeli fire" was ABC's Findlay (October 1). In addition, NBC anchor John Siegenthaler twisted the meaning of the report by his own correspondent, Tom Aspell. Siegenthaler prefaced Aspell's

report with this summary: "Israeli troops opened
fire, killing twelve people, including a twelve-
year-old boy caught in the crossfire" (September
30). But Aspell reported only that the boy had
died in a crossfire, not that the fatal shots had
come from the Israelis. Four days after the tragic
event, most of the other news organizations abandoned their agnosticism and stated or implied
that the shots that had killed the boy had indeed
come from the Israelis (*New York Times, Washington Post,* Fox, October 4). The reason for this
shift was not hard to find. As the Associated
Press's Laura King reported in a story carried in
the *Post,* "The [Israeli] Army acknowledged later
that its soldiers apparently fired the fatal shots
and expressed sorrow" (October 4).

After the early acceptance of responsibility
by the Israeli spokesman, the Israeli army or-
dered a formal investigation, and several months
later it concluded that its soldiers probably had
not fired the fatal shots. This conclusion was
subsequently reinforced by an investigative program broadcast in March 2002 by the German television network ARD.[4] While most of the rocks and
Molotov cocktails were thrown from the direction
of the intersection where the rioters had massed,
a pair of apartment buildings used as barracks by
Palestinian policemen stood behind the Israeli
outpost, and some of the shooting on the Palestinian side came from those buildings. Shots directed from there at the Israeli outpost would
have been on a line that led to the intersection
where Mohammed and his father were crouching.
These and other details about the shooting (e.g.,
the facts that Israeli weapons have better sights,
that Israeli fire tends to be more disciplined
than that of the Palestinians, who are less trained,
and that Mohammed and his father were not amid any
group of shooters or stone throwers) led the German crew to conclude that the Palestinian barracks were a more likely source of the fire that
killed Mohammed than the Israeli position.

Because the Palestinian hospital where Mohammed and his father were taken claimed to have recovered not a single one of the roughly dozen bullets that hit the two, it will never be known which side's fire killed Mohammed. But the incident, which is likely to live forever in Palestinian lore, also symbolizes a profound asymmetry in the public relations activities of the two sides. The Israelis had acknowledged culpability, on the basis of superficial information, for a shooting that they later concluded (plausibly) had not been done by them. In contrast, the Palestinians never acknowledged a shred of doubt in fixing the blame on the other side and making the shooting out to have been deliberate, when in truth, even if the fire did come from Israeli guns, it almost certainly was accidental, the boy having been a bystander to violent demonstrations. Yet, PA chairman Yasir Arafat's top advisor, Nabil Abu Rudeineh, told the *Times,* "This is a killing in cold blood, an attack on an innocent child without any excuse. This cannot be forgiven" (Orme, October 1).

In a similar vein, referring to the rioters who died from Israeli gunfire during those few days, Arafat lieutenant Nabil Sha'ath accused the Israelis of "premeditated murder" (CBS, September 30; NBC, *Washington Post* [Hockstader], October 1). Chief Palestinian negotiator Saeb Erekat, sounding a theme that was to be repeated often over the next two years, stated, "It's a massacre being committed against the Palestinian people . . . a complete massacre" (NBC, October 1; *Washington Post* [Hockstader], October 3). Ironically, if there was a single deadly shooting "in cold blood" or "premeditated murder" during these first days of the intifada, it was the killing of the Israeli policeman by his Palestinian partner in Qalqilya on September 29.

In short, while Israeli spokesmen seemed to strive to provide truthful answers even while straining to put their nation's best foot forward, Palestinian spokesmen conducted themselves as if

they felt no similar constraint. Yet, in the apparent interest of evenhandedness, the news organizations reported the two sides' claims equally
and gave every appearance of treating them with
equal credulity. A rare departure from this occurred when Sharon, defending his visit to the
mount, pointed out that any Arab was free to visit
the Israeli Holocaust memorial, Yad Vashem, a
site of great sensitivity to Jews. In reporting
Sharon's point, the *Times*' Sontag followed it with
a rebuttal of her own, reminding readers that "Yad
Vashem is not a religious site" (October 2). No-
where in the stories reviewed for this study did
she rebut the arguments of any Palestinian spokesman
she quoted.

Despite Erekat's continued insistence that all
the shooting was on one side, by October 1, virtually all major U.S. news organizations were
reporting that the confrontations involved gunfire from the Palestinians as well. Still, there
were numerous reports echoing the Palestinian accusation that the Israelis were using disproportionate force. And Israeli denials were sometimes
brushed aside in odd non sequiturs. For example,
CNN's Mike Hanna reported: "Israel says its forces
are using lethal force only when Israeli lives
are at risk. But Amnesty International and other
independent organizations record that the overwhelming majority of . . . wounded are Palestinian" (October 2). The word "but" suggested that
the second sentence nullifies the first, but it
does not. Similarly, the *Times*' Orme discounted
the Israeli version of the scene at Netzarim junction without directly contradicting it: "Israeli
Army spokesmen said the troops came under live
fire from the Palestinian police. But television
footage of the incident, including the shooting
of the 12-year-old boy, and the absence of any
serious Israeli casualties, served to reinforce
the Palestinians' belief that the Israelis were
responding with disproportionate force" (October
1). Additional film footage that circulated as
the al-Dura story reverberated indeed showed many

Molotov cocktails hitting the Israeli post and much Palestinian fire.

Three days later, the *Times* carried a feature story by Orme on "the case being made here by Palestinians and some Israelis here, as well as by diplomats abroad, that Israeli forces have employed deadly force too readily" (October 4). Orme claimed that "there are many documented instances of close-range shooting at eye level," although he did not explain how they were "documented." The *Post*'s Hockstader also wrote about the second day's violence that "Palestinian officials [stated] at least seven people . . . had been hit in the eye by Israeli bullets" (September 30). Were Israeli marksmen trained to aim for the eyes? And was their fire so accurate? These claims cried out for verification before being reported.

episode 2:

Barak's Ultimatum

During the second week of the al-Aqsa intifada, few foresaw that it might continue for a long time. The peace process had endured for seven years, and a week of mayhem, however upsetting, seemed an anomaly. The week was highlighted by three things: a public ultimatum issued by Prime Minister Ehud Barak warning the Palestinians that failure to end the intifada would lead to a harsher Israeli response; the destruction of a Jewish holy place, Joseph's Tomb in Nablus; and bloodshed inside Israel's 1967 borders, where thirteen Arabs died in clashes between Jewish and Arab Israelis. Much of the reportage aimed at discovering the underlying dynamics and causes of all this unexpected violence.

Israel's version was that the violence was initiated by the Palestinians and that it was fomented, if not directed, by Yasir Arafat. This was the reasoning behind Barak's ultimatum. In contrast, the Palestinians claimed that Israel had attacked them largely unprovoked, was continuing to attack them, and was employing excessive force. This indictment was somewhat inconsistent in that the concept of "excessive force" seems to imply that some lesser amount of force might have been appropriate, implicitly conceding that Israel was responding to provocation. If Israel was engaged in naked aggression, as the Palestinian spokesmen usually suggested, then the use of force was illegitimate per se, regardless of its level.

Despite Barak's warning, Palestinian spokesmen described Israeli action in terms suggesting that it was already so severe that it could scarcely be intensified. According to the *Washington Post* (Keith Richburg, October 5, 2000), Arafat claimed that a "serious massacre" was "being perpetrated against the Palestinian people." On CNN, Palestinian spokeswoman Hanan Ashrawi stated that Israel's army was waging a "unilateral war against the civilian popu-

lation" (October 7), while Saeb Erekat again stated
that "Palestinians are being massacred" (October
9). Ashrawi also appeared on NBC, proclaiming an-
grily that "a whole nation is being killed every
day and being asked to lie back and to die quietly,
not even to defend themselves" (October 8).

What did the various news outlets say about
the causes of the continuing violence? In the *New
York Times,* William Orme and Jane Perlez reported
that Arafat "said he was willing to resume peace
talks, but 'first we must stop the massacres against
our people'" (October 6). They added that "the
radical Islamic movement Hamas . . . bitterly
chastised Mr. Arafat for negotiating while the
violence continued," which made Arafat seem something of a beleaguered peace-seeker. Yet, their
explanation of Hamas's position was strange since
Hamas was neither against violence nor in favor
of negotiations. It proclaimed its goal to be the
destruction of Israel and its belief, accord-
ingly, in "armed struggle" as the means to attain
that goal. Orme and Perlez offered no explication
for their odd report. In the same story, they
wrote that "the Israelis have refused an international commission, arguing it could prove . . .
unsympathetic to Israeli security interests." This,
too, was an odd formulation, for Israel's pro-
fessed fear was not that a commission might find
fault with Israel but that it might be so prejudiced at the outset as to guarantee a one-sided
conclusion. The word "biased" rather than "unsympathetic" would have conveyed Israel's position more accurately.

Two days later, the *Times'* Sunday "Week in Review" section carried a 1,200-word piece by John
Kifner devoted to debunking "the underlying assumption—shared by Israeli officials who accused
Mr. Arafat of 'orchestrating' the violence— . . .
that he had the power to swiftly turn [it] off"
(October 8). Kifner quoted an anonymous "Western
expert" who stated that "Arafat's authority has
eroded over the years," adding that "there is a

tremendous frustration among Palestinians . . .
an awful lot of rage" as a result of "the perception . . . that the Israelis want to drag the
process out, to build new settlements [and] ex-
pand existing ones." Kifner also quoted Israeli
dissident Meron Benvenisti, who scorned the view
that Arafat was in charge as "a typical approach
of Israeli . . . so-called Arab experts." And
Kifner concluded with quotes from a young member
of the Tanzim, the Palestinian group that was
initiating much of the violence, saying "the Israelis think that Arafat controls us like pup-
pets . . . but we are a force on our own." Kifner
did not see fit to quote anyone with a view contrary to his own thesis.

Washington Post news columns also conveyed
doubts about Israel's view that Arafat was responsible for the violence. "Many suspect that with
emotions running so high, Arafat may not be able
to halt the violence even if he wants to," reported Lee Hockstader (October 7). Hockstader went
on to explain:

> The Palestinians' sense of grievance is bound up
> in long-standing and unmet demands—for an inde-
> pendent state with East Jerusalem as its capi-
> tal; for the return of refugees who fled or were
> forced from their homes in Israel's 1948 War of
> Independence; for the release of prisoners held
> for years in Israeli jails; and for the return
> of West Bank and Gaza territories captured by
> Israel in the 1967 Middle East war.

The question of what, exactly, the Palestinians
were fighting for was a crucial one. And the
interpretation Hockstader introduced here—that
the Palestinians were after a return of the territories Israel captured in 1967—was to be repeated often in *Post* coverage over the next two
years, although it was tendentious. Most Ameri-
cans and Europeans, even most Israelis, believed
that these territories, or the larger part of
them, should be given over to the Palestinians.
If this was indeed the Palestinians' goal, then

there was much reason to sympathize with them. If, however, their goal was to destroy Israel, then the Palestinians' struggle would deserve less sympathy.

Alas, there was much evidence that the Palestinians had not abandoned the aim of ruling all of mandatory Palestine, including the parts that constituted Israel within its pre-1967 borders. In public opinion polls, a plurality of Palestinians stated that this was their goal, and the official Palestinian Authority (PA) maps and textbooks invariably portrayed "Palestine" as encompassing Israel proper as well as the occupied territories. This, too, was the implication of the demand for the return of the 1948 refugees mentioned by Hockstader without any explication. The return of these refugees and their progeny, or all the millions who claimed such status, would suffice to ensure that Israel would no longer be a majority Jewish state. In short, Hockstader and several of his colleagues who used similar language were putting their own benign spin on the intifada. Eventually, the *Post*'s ombudsman acknowledged that objections to this formulation constituted a "fair criticism of its reportage."[5] But the paper's correspondents ignored his assessment; they went on using such language with undiminished regularity.

Hockstader was also on shaky ground in his reference to "prisoners held for years in Israeli jails." Such prisoners had indeed been a sensitive issue in the Oslo negotiations, but in the end Israel had released them all, even those guilty of murder. The Palestinians in Israeli jails at the time of Hockstader's article were those who had been incarcerated for new acts of violence perpetrated after Oslo.

While Hockstader's summary of Palestinian goals put them in a favorable light, his description of Israeli actions was far from sympathetic. "Instead of a deft tap," he reported, Prime Minister Barak "has authorized firepower that is being criticized

as indiscriminate and excessive. . . . Television
footage of Israeli soldiers using tear gas, rubber-coated bullets, antitank weapons and helicopter gunships against armed and unarmed rioters has
generated a storm of criticism that Barak has gone
too far" (October 9). Later in the article, Hockstader
added, "Mustafa Barghouti, a Palestinian physician
who heads a medical association in the West Bank,
accused Israel of employing a heavily disproportionate use of force. 'I don't think they need those
kind of weapons to protect their own troops,' he
said. 'They're so well equipped, so well protected.'"
Hockstader's citing of Barghouti was misleading.
Medical personnel are universally respected, and
while they may, as individuals, have a loyalty to
their own side, they are nonetheless, as profes-
sionals, often presumed to have a degree of objectivity. *Post* readers had no way of knowing that
Barghouti, while he may be a physician, serves
primarily as a Palestinian political leader (he
was, for example, a member of the Palestinian del-
egation to the 1991 Madrid peace conference) and
was presented as such in numerous citations by
other journalists.

Reinforcing the image of a heartless Israel in
another story, Hockstader wrote on October 5:

> Some Israelis have Arab acquaintances but few
> have Arab friends, and the mounting death toll
> among Palestinians has registered with most Is-
> raelis more as a statistic than as individual
> human tragedies. 'Our deaths are stories, but
> theirs are just numbers,' said the headline on an
> unusually frank article in the Israeli newspaper
> *Haaretz* this week.

The essence of Hockstader's assertion—that Israelis are callous to Palestinian suffering—is im-
pressionistic and cannot be proved or disproved,
but his reference to the *Ha'aretz* article was
misleading. *Ha'aretz* is the flagship of the lib-
eral side of the Israeli spectrum, and for it to
carry articles that are self-critical from an
Israeli perspective is anything but "unusual."

This illustrates one of the several asymmetries in the Arab-Israeli news environment. Israel has numerous publications and journalists that are sharply critical of their own government's policies, and even those that are pro-government share with the presses of other democracies an ethos of seeking and reporting the truth even if it is embarrassing to their own side. Many of the stories in the Western press that put Israel on the defensive originate in the Israeli press. Nothing comparable exists on the Arab side.

On the television news, only the occasional broadcast suggested an explanation for the violence. On October 9, ABC correspondent Gillian Findlay reported that

> Palestinian leaders say they have been trying to rein in the gunmen but they also warn that as long as Israeli troops keep killing Palestinians there will be little anyone can do. 'Israel started this war,' said security chief Muhammad Dahlan today, 'everything Israel is doing is making Palestinian anger stronger.'

Neither Findlay nor anchor Peter Jennings said a word to cast doubt on the claim that Israel was the initiator of the violence, nor did they balance Dahlan with any Israeli spokesman who might have contradicted him. On the contrary, as if to give credence to the image of Israelis as unprovoked aggressors, Findlay went on to say that "there are reports of Israeli helicopters opening fire on civilian homes in Hebron." She did not explain further, although it is hard to imagine that this report of a report was accurate unless the helicopters were returning fire. There was no similar report from the other outlets examined in this study.

ABC also lent more credence than any other outlet to the charge that Israel was employing excessive force. Findlay reported: "The Israelis say they are practicing restraint, but at this hospital, doctors say they are still seeing plenty of evidence of live ammunition, plenty of evi-

dence the soldiers are still shooting to kill—
chest wounds, head wounds" (October 6). This made
it sound as if Israel's claims were false, but why
should the accounts of the Palestinian doctors be
taken at face value, as Findlay seemed to take
them? And what were those individuals doing at
the time they were shot? If they were shooting at
the Israelis, then were the Israelis to be faulted
for firing back?

By this time, many news reports had verified
Israel's complaints that Palestinian gunmen were
firing from amid the mobs of youthful stone throwers.
Yet, in another report, Findlay seemed to cast
doubt on this: "In Gaza, Israeli soldiers opened
fire on schoolboys throwing stones" (October 10).
Did she mean to assert that no gunmen were among
the "schoolboys"? If so, how could she have known
this? On still another occasion she reported, "In
Gaza, Israeli troops blew up two Palestinian apartment buildings, buildings they say Palestinian gunmen
had been using for cover" (October 8). She did not
say—as, for example, Keith Richburg reported in
the *Washington Post*—that the two "apartment buildings" in fact served as barracks for the Palestinian security forces. Nor was it merely Israel's
contention that gunmen operated from those buildings: footage of shooting from them had been shown
on the air. Indeed, it was from those buildings
that the fatal shots that killed young Mohammed al-
Dura had probably been fired, according to the
assessment of the German television broadcast mentioned in "episode 1" of this study.[6]

On October 9, NBC correspondent Andrea Mitchell's
explanation of the violence offered a novel twist:

> To many, peace seemed so close at Camp David in
> July. How did it all fall apart? First, Pales-
> tinian resentment on the street, people see no
> economic rewards . . . and they resent the U.S.
> for blaming Arafat when the summit collapses
> while praising Israel's Prime Minister Barak.

In other words, the fault lay not with Arafat for
refusing to negotiate at Camp David but with

President Bill Clinton for criticizing Arafat's refusal.

CNN was the other network to lend support to the accusation that Israel was using excessive force. When the United States abstained on a United Nations (UN) Security Council resolution critical of Israel, Mike Hanna explained that it was "a pointed gesture from the United States towards the Israelis that activities within the last week have become virtually indefensible" (October 7). But Hanna's version was at odds with the explanation given by U.S. officials. UN ambassador Richard Holbrooke stated that the resolution had evoked his "clear distaste," but that "vetoing it would have created . . . further problems in the region for us as the honest broker and negotiator."[7]

On October 7, CNN ran a string of interviews, all from one side. First, correspondent Mike Hanna spent four minutes on camera with Palestinian negotiator Saeb Erekat, who said that the underlying motive behind Barak's ultimatum was that he wanted an "exit strategy from the peace process." Hanna did not press Erekat on why that might be, an obvious question in view of the fact that Barak had staked his leadership on the peace process. This was followed by an equally long interview of Palestinian spokeswoman Ashrawi, who claimed that the "Israeli army" was waging a "unilateral war against the civilian population." This, too, passed unchallenged by the interviewer, Wolf Blitzer. Following Ashrawi, CNN brought on John Daly of the Middle East Institute, a Saudi-funded Washington think tank. Daly criticized Barak and Sharon but not Arafat or any other Palestinian, and he called for turning the whole problem over to the UN. As against these three Arab or pro-Arab spokesmen, no one on that evening's news presented Israel's side of the argument.

The next evening, CNN treated viewers to the silliest media moment in this mostly unfunny episode. The lead-in to that evening's report stated,

"Unrest in the Middle East has spread to other Arab nations. Thousands marched in Baghdad, Iraq, Sunday to condemn Israel." Could the network have been unaware that, under the iron-fisted rule of Saddam Husayn, spontaneous political demonstrations did not occur in Baghdad? When thousands marched against Israel (or for any other reason), it was because they were ordered to march. The last thing in the world this march bespoke was "unrest."

That week was also witness to one of the more important exercises of media self-policing. On October 7 the *Times* ran a story clarifying an erroneous photo caption it had published during the first days of violence. The photo showed a dazed victim, blood streaming down his face, whom the caption identified as a Palestinian sitting near an armed Israeli soldier. In fact, the injured man was a Jewish American student, Tuvia Grossman of Chicago, who, together with two friends, had been pulled from a taxi in Arab Jerusalem by a mob that attempted to beat them to death by battering their heads with stones. They had escaped, albeit injured, to the protection of the Israeli soldier pictured in the photo. The caption falsely describing Grossman as a Palestinian had been attached to the photo distributed by the Associated Press and was carried by many newspapers in addition to the *Times*. Whatever fault the *Times* bore in having run the caption and then a brief, insufficiently enlightening correction a few days later was counterbalanced by the full account of the story the *Times* gave on October 7. One can only wonder how many of the other papers that used the misleading caption corrected it as carefully as the *Times* did.

One wonders, too, how the Associated Press's error came about in the first place. Certainly it was not deliberate, but could it be that the overriding theme of Palestinian victimhood was coloring the lens through which reporters were viewing events? Were it not for the need to correct the earlier caption, the story of the assault on Grossman and his friends would never have run (it ran a week after the event). Was not a murderous mob attack on innocent Jewish American bystanders newsworthy? Aside from the effort by the *Times* to set the record straight on the caption, scarcely a story on acts of violence by Arab rioters against Jewish civilians appeared in the outlets reviewed for this study. Were there none?

The one exception was on October 6, when both CBS and NBC offered brief but vivid footage of Arab rioters on the Temple Mount once again showering stones and bottles on Jewish worshipers at the Wailing Wall below. In contrast, CNN showed Israeli security personnel charging onto the mount in response to these attacks. "Israeli police stormed a bitterly contested holy site, tearing down Palestinian flags," reported Judy Woodruff. But she offered neither a mention nor a view of the assault on the Jewish worshipers that precipitated the charge. No mention of these stonings was found to appear in the other media outlets reviewed for this study.

Coverage of another kind of anti-Jewish attack was also uneven, the destruction of Joseph's Tomb, a prayer site for orthodox Jews that the Oslo Accords stated should remain under the protection of Israeli forces. (As with many ancient sites, there is uncertainty about whether this was the actual site of Joseph's burial.) A shrine had been erected, and holy books were kept there for use in prayer. As it was located in Nablus, a densely populated Palestinian area, it became a flashpoint. Israel withdrew its forces from the site after the PA agreed to protect it, but it was trashed and burned soon after the Israeli departure. The *Washington Post,* in a dispatch from Richburg, carried a lengthier and more descriptive account of the "dismantling" of the tomb "brick by brick" (October 8) than did the *New York Times,* which mentioned it only briefly, although adding a photo. Of particular interest was Richburg's description of some of the participants:

> 'I feel proud,' said Nasser Badawi, 35, a militiaman from Yasser Arafat's Fatah organization, who wore a gray T-shirt and had a shiny mini-AK-47 assault rifle slung across his back. He said he began pelting Israeli soldiers with rocks when he was 15 years old and only last week was able to fire on them with his automatic weapon. 'I feel like we did something today,' he said. 'This is victory.'

This account of the role of Arafat's own organization in the mayhem might have cast some light on the question of Arafat's role (that is, whether he was encouraging the violence or helpless to rein it in), yet no other news organization except NBC reported it, and even the *Post,* in other stories, did not seem to give much weight to the implications.

A few days later, the *Times*' Orme reported that "[t]he Palestinians invited observers to their hasty restoration work at Joseph's tomb" (October 11). Orme did not say whether he had accepted the invitation, and his story carried no description suggesting that he had been there, so it remained unclear whether any restoration had occurred. As it turned out, "restoration" was in fact performed: the building was transformed into a mosque.[8]

NBC correspondent Ron Allen provided a vivid account of the events at the tomb, including the fact that Palestinian police stood by passively during the destruction despite the PA's pledges. A day later, he also reported a retaliatory action that occurred at a mosque in the Israeli city of Tiberias. "A band of young men burned and looted this Moslem place of worship," he stated (October 7). The mosque was an old one, no longer in use, so it is unclear what "looted" may have meant. Fox and ABC also reported both events, with ABC's Gillian Findlay telling viewers that "angry Israelis attacked and burned two of the city's mosques" (October 8). No correspondent other than Findlay reported multiple mosque burnings in Tiberias— and for good reason. There is only one mosque in Tiberias: the old, unused one. The town's population is almost entirely Jewish. No mention of either the Tiberias or the Joseph's Tomb attacks was found on CBS. CNN mentioned the attack on the tomb but only belatedly, in the context of Jerrold Kessel's report that "under Mr. Arafat's orders, repairs began on the Jewish shrine" (October 10).

Following the mosque report, Findlay showed an angry crowd of Israeli demonstrators. She translated their chants as "Death to the Arabs" and "We want blood." She then put on a single, threatening sentence from an interview with Barak: "Under the right of self-defense we will know what to do and how to act, how to respond, how to initiate those types [of action] that are needed." Then she switched to Saeb Erekat, who lamented "a very ugly scene" and appealed for the international community to "stop this madness and to stop hell from breaking loose." Comparing the view she offered of the two leaders, her audience would have been likely to conclude that it was the Palestinian side that was appalled by violence.

The arson attack in Tiberias was not the only violence within Israel. Arab Israelis in the northern part of the country rioted and blocked roads in support of their brethren in the territories. This led to deadly confrontations with police, and it also led to counter-riots by angry Jews who at one point swooped down from the Jewish town of Upper Nazareth into the Arab town of Nazareth, raining destruction. On October 10, *New York Times* correspondent Chris Hedges reported:

> When the police arrived, they found groups of Israeli Arabs backed into alleys and throwing rocks at the Jewish demonstrators who were attacking the Arab area. The police pulled the Jewish protesters across the road and fired on the Arab crowd, shooting [two] dead.

That same day in the *Washington Post*, Richburg
wrote:

> Hundreds of Jewish civilians from a nearby town
> arrived . . . firing automatic weapons and bran-
> dishing clubs. Residents say they shouted 'death
> to the Arabs!' Two Arab citizens of Israel were
> killed. . . . Fifty others were injured. . . .
> Even for many here who are accustomed to the
> violence and invective, the attack by Jews against
> the Arabs of Nazareth was considered astonishing
> and difficult to explain.

And on October 9, CNN's Jerrold Kessel relayed

> ominous reports . . . of more violence and riot-
> ing inside Israel . . . and by Jewish settlers on
> the West Bank against Palestinians there. But
> Jewish Israelis have taken to attacking Arab Is-
> raelis in various parts of the country. . . .
> [L]ast night in the town of Nazareth . . . two
> Israeli Arab citizens shot dead. . . . Minds and
> hearts have really been hardening . . . both in
> the streets of Ramallah and Gaza and now very
> much in the streets of Israel, as Jewish Israelis
> are taking on their fellow citizens, Arabs, and
> attacking them literally.

On ABC, anchor Peter Jennings stated, "Last night,
two more Palestinians were killed by the Israelis
in northern Israel, which led to demonstrations
today in Palestinian towns, which led to confrontations with the Israeli army again" (October 9).
And CBS's Richard Roth stated, "The nightmare has
been a series of attacks on Israel's unnoticed
minority" (October 11). The latter cliché seemed
particularly inapt in an atmosphere thick with
discourse about the "demographic factor" in the
political struggle. Of all these accounts, only
that of Hedges in the *Times* suggested that the
Jewish riots were in response to provocation on the
part of the Arab Israelis. Viewers of CNN or ABC
would not have known that the two men who died were
shot by police, not by the Jewish rioters.

Meanwhile, violence continued in the West Bank
and Gaza, and there were several incidents in

which doubtful claims were made by Palestinians, and not just the leadership. In the *Post,* Richburg wrote, "Palestinians reported that a 9-year-old boy, identified as Mohammed Abu Assi, also was killed at Netzarim junction, shot in the chest during clashes" (October 5). But Richburg went on to say that "the Israeli military denied its troops fired the bullet that killed the boy, saying it had investigated the incident with the help of Palestinian officials." Netzarim junction was the spot where Mohammed al-Dura had died five days before. Had a second shooting of a still younger child by the Israelis in fact occurred, it seems all but certain that it would have received far more publicity.

In another dubious incident, Fox's David Lee Miller reported that "near . . . Ramallah a Palestinian man was found beaten to death" (October 9). The next day's *Washington Post* carried a fuller report by Richburg: "Two Palestinians were found dead this morning on the West Bank, apparently killed by Jewish settlers—or so the Palestinians believe. One . . . appeared to have been tortured and his mutilated body had been set on fire." While Richburg's phrase "so the Palestinians believe" established a modicum of reportorial distance, the reasons for such distance became clear only in the *New York Times* account that same day. There, correspondent Deborah Sontag reported that Palestinian

> protesters and mourners became enraged by the announcement of an alleged brutal killing of a Palestinian by settlers. The 40-year-old man's skull was crushed, his bones broken and his body burned, the crowd was told. Palestinian television repeatedly showed pictures of the charred and mutilated body . . . and offered the opinion of some Palestinian officials that the killing justified an open season on settlers.

Two paragraphs later, Sontag added this enlightening note: "Israeli military officials, however, disputed the account of how the man had died.

They contend that the man, Isam Hamad, 36, died
in a car crash north of Ramallah and that the
Palestinians chose to exploit the terrible con-
dition of his body."

The oddest treatment of this incident was seen
on CNN. On October 9, Ben Wedeman reported the
Palestinian allegation that the victim had been
killed by Israeli settlers and also reported that
the Israeli authorities had investigated the death
and discovered that the man had died in an auto-
mobile accident. Nonetheless, a night later Mike
Hanna reported the story again, in a manner lend-
ing credence to the Palestinian claims. From the
Ramallah hospital he stated:

> Displayed here [are] pictures of the body. . . .
> According to the doctors, the man had been burnt
> with some kind of electrical implement as well
> as cigarettes. The X rays of his head indicate
> he was then beaten with heavy objects. The doc-
> tors here say he appeared to have been murdered.
> Now the Israelis claim that he was killed in a
> car accident.

Then Hanna turned to a doctor who stated, pointing
to the pictures, "Look, you see. This is a car
accident?" The net effect was to cast doubt on
the Israeli version, not the Palestinian version, although it was the latter that was almost certainly fictitious.

episode 3:

The Ramallah
Lynching

On October 12, 2000, as
the intifada began its
third week, two Israeli
reservists on their way to duty in the West Bank
took a wrong turn and ended up amid a hostile
crowd in Ramallah. Shortly thereafter at the
Ramallah police station, they were murdered by
the mob. Later that day, Israel retaliated by
firing rockets into the by-then-empty police station and a few other sites. The reports of these
traumatic events varied greatly in their tone and
emphasis.

The most vivid account was provided by Deborah
Sontag in the *New York Times* on October 13. "Israeli helicopter gunships rocketed Ramallah and
Gaza City today after a Palestinian mob here stabbed
and stomped to death two Israeli reserve soldiers
and then paraded a mutilated body through town,"
began the story. It added:

> Before the rockets started falling, Palestinian
> youths danced on the bloody spot where one Is-
> raeli was tossed through floral curtains into
> the mob below. In a call and response, they
> chanted: 'Here is where we gouged his eyes! Here
> is where we ripped off his legs! Here is where we
> smashed in his face!' One teenage boy joyously
> thrust in the air the oil dipstick from the
> charred carcass of the soldiers' car, which had
> been burnt by the mob and lay curled beneath a
> billboard that said, 'Rule of Law Project.'

In contrast, the *Washington Post* account by Keith
Richburg was much milder. It began by explaining
the context. "Like so many days here, this one
began with a funeral" (October 13). The Palestinians were "grieving and angry." Only in the fifth
paragraph did it get around to the murder, and
then with none of the grisly detail to be found
in the *Times*. The sixth paragraph consisted of a
single sentence, isolated for emphasis. "The Israeli government's reaction was swift and harsh."
Then the article quoted the ubiquitous Mustafa
Barghouti—identifying him only as "a Palestinian

doctor in Ramallah," although he is in fact a spokesman and political leader—claiming that twenty-five people were injured, nineteen of them civilians, and adding "this is a massacre." The *Post* did not mention, as the *Times* had, that Israel gave the Palestinian Authority advance warning of its retaliatory strike so that the buildings could be emptied.

In the aftermath of the murders, Palestinians sought to extenuate them by claiming that the two soldiers were suspected of being Israeli under-cover agents. Such agents do in fact infiltrate Palestinian areas, but these two were pulled from a car bearing Israeli license plates and were clothed in their military uniforms, which made the claim absurd. Nonetheless, the *Post*'s Nora Boustany lent credence to it by reporting falsely that "at least some of" the reservists "were in civilian clothing" (October 13).

On October 14, both the *Times* (twice, in articles by Hedges/Perlez and Sontag) and the *Post* (Richburg) reported that Arafat had or-dered a "very serious investigation" of the kill-ings. In fact, no investigation appears to have taken place except by Israel, which some days later arrested a number of men believed to have been the perpetrators.

On ABC, Peter Jennings—who, on nights when Arabs had died, introduced the story with short declarative sentences about Arabs "killed by Is-raelis" as if to drive home the point that the circumstances were secondary—took a very differ-ent tack in this case. His preliminary sound bite was painstakingly evenhanded: "Israelis and Pal-estinians, another day of dead and wounded, each side accuses the other of going to war" (October 12). Then his lead-in was longer than usual, care-fully painting the context:

> It has been another terrible day of fighting between Israelis and Palestinians. There was a particularly ugly incident in the Palestin-ian city of Ramallah. Forty-thousand people

live there. This week they're all angry at the
Israelis. There was about to be another funeral. Thousands of young men had congregated.
At least two Israeli army reservists were
clearly in the wrong place. They were stopped
and taken into a police station. That was not
enough for their protection.

Correspondent Gillian Findlay then reported the
murders and the retaliation, devoting an equal
number of lines to each, after which Jennings
added this exquisitely balanced homily: "There
are Israelis and Palestinians who do not want
this peace plan to succeed. Yasir Arafat is vul-
nerable to those forces and so is Prime Minister
Barak."

There was, however, a lot that was question-
able about the equivalence that Jennings drew
here. Barak was elected to his post in a parliamentary system, indeed, one known for the short
life spans of its governments, whereas Arafat had
ruled the Palestinian movement for more than thirty
years (and had been elected president of the
Palestinian Authority without meaningful opposition). It was true that Arafat was susceptible to
internal political pressures, as is any authoritarian leader, but this is not equivalent to the
situation of a parliamentary leader. Moreover,
Barak had staked all his political chips on a
peace settlement. He had tabled an offer embody-
ing concessions that went well beyond anything
that a majority in Israel's parliament had said
it would support. His political strategy was apparent: if the Palestinians would agree to a
settlement, he believed that the Israeli public
would be so happy with the breakthrough that all
demurrals about the terms of peace would be swept
away. Arafat, on the other hand, had turned down
the American compromises proposed at Camp David
without even deigning to suggest an alternative,
and, as the intifada proceeded, he was refusing
to call for an end to the violence. So, while
Jennings's words were literally true, the im-

pression they conveyed that the continuing violence was equally the will of the two sides was
false.

Jennings then closed the segment with a report
that carried his exercise in equivalence to the
level of outright concoction. "And as everybody
in the region has said today, nobody knows what
will happen tomorrow. Various Palestinian fac-
tions as well as Jewish settlers in the territories are calling for another day of rage," he
stated. The Palestinian groups did in fact often
proclaim "days of rage," but the settlers, although guilty of occasional acts of violence, did
nothing of the sort.

This strange insertion of the settlers into
Jennings's report harkened back to his broadcast
of the previous evening, when he had told viewers, "There are now more than a hundred Jewish
settlements in the Palestinian territories, and
the settlers, the Jewish settlers, are now very
involved in the violence" (October 11). This led
into Findlay's report:

> Ever since Rabbi Hillel Lieberman's bullet-ridden
> body was found three days ago, Jewish settlers
> have been talking revenge. Today, thousands of
> them turned out for the funeral and a procession
> that took them right past a Palestinian town.
> The settlers say the Palestinians threw the first
> stones, but soon the settlers were on a rampage.
> Attacking Palestinian homes, then turning on a
> truck driven by Palestinians. Israeli soldiers
> accompanying the convoy did little to stop the
> mob. It wasn't long before shots rang out from
> Palestinians hiding in the hills, the army says,
> and the soldiers began firing back. . . . Today,
> the army sent tanks to defend the settlers. The
> real worry is the settlers may go on the attack.

When word of the desecration of Joseph's Tomb had
spread, Hillel Lieberman, an orthodox Jew in his
thirties, had set off by foot to investigate it.
He was apparently intercepted and murdered by
Palestinians. Although reported elsewhere, this
was not mentioned on ABC's evening news until

Findlay's remark. Only the "rampage" of Jewish settlers, in which no one died or even seemed to have been seriously injured, impelled ABC to note Lieberman's murder.

On October 13, Jennings continued this tack. He prefaced that evening's broadcast with the question: "What does a day of rage mean between Israelis and Palestinians?" He did not repeat his previous claim that Jewish settlers had, like Palestinians, proclaimed a "day of rage." Indeed the broadcast contained nothing about the settlers, presumably because there had been no action that day on their part. Still, Jennings labored to preserve his tendentious equation by observing that "rage [is] felt by both Israelis and Palestinians." But the example of Jewish "rage" that he presented was nothing of the kind. He reported: "And today in Jerusalem, Israeli security forces barred Palestinians under the age of forty-five from praying at the al-Aqsa mosque. So, young Palestinians prayed outside, and some young men were chased and beaten by Israeli police, which may help make clear why arranging a summit is so difficult."

The reason young men had been barred from the Friday prayers was that these occasions had repeatedly turned into riots, with rocks and bottles being tossed down on the Jewish worshipers at the Wailing Wall beneath. Nor was the action of the Israeli police an expression of "rage" (although the officers may have been angry), but rather a method of chasing away young men who had defied the ban. The claim that this event explained the difficulty of renewing negotiations was disingenuous since it was Arafat who at this point was standing in the way.

CNN's Christiane Amanpour reported from the region that week, placing great stress on what she made clear she believed was the excessive use of force by Israel. In an interview with one Israeli cabinet minister, she pressed: "Even the supporters of Prime Minister Barak are saying that he's just gone too far this time, that there simply is

too much force being used against stone throwers"
(October 10). What was striking about this was the
phrase "even the supporters." If the prime minister
had come from Israel's hardline camp, then the
assertion would have been coherent, but Barak was
very much a dove. It was not clear whom Amanpour
was referencing, if anyone or anything at all other
than her own feelings. But if she meant that some
of the most dovish Israelis criticized Barak's use
of force (few in reality did), then her phrase
still made little sense since there would have been
nothing remarkable about their stance.

Later in the same broadcast, she mentioned
some acts of violence that had occurred inside
Israel proper, perpetrated by Jews against Arab
Israelis: "A new sort of ugly dimension has come
into this: Jewish settlers turning on Israeli
citizens who happen to be Arabs." This was a
further muddle. The settlers were not in Israel
proper but in the territories, and the Arabs
there were not Israeli citizens. The violence
inside Israel's 1967 borders did not have anything to do with settlers. While Amanpour be-
trayed strong opinions about the conflict, she
seemed strangely deficient in the most elementary background knowledge.

episode 4:

The Sharm
al-Shaykh Summit

On October 16 and 17, 2000, the leaders of Israel, Jordan, Egypt, the United States, and the Palestinian Authority held a summit in Sharm al-Shaykh, Egypt, initiated by President Bill Clinton in the hope of arresting the Middle East violence and salvaging the peace process. Israel agreed to the Palestinians' key demand, the creation of an international fact-finding mission, insisting, however, that it be under American aegis. This became the Mitchell Commission (so called after its chair, former senator George Mitchell). Israel also agreed to a simultaneous stand-down from violent confrontations rather than, as it had proposed, a pullback of its forces only in response to a Palestinian cessation of violence. But Yasir Arafat issued no call for an end to violence, and the *Washington Post* reported within an hour after the summit's end that Marwan Barghouti, "the fiery field marshal of the Palestinian revolt, had declared, 'we will continue'" (Lee Hockstader, October 18).

The Palestinians' determination to continue what they called their "uprising" came across more vividly in Hockstader's report than in any account by the other outlets reviewed for this study. Yet, he once again referred to it as a "revolt against Israel's continued occupation of most of the West Bank and some of the Gaza Strip," although, as mentioned previously, as good a case could be made for calling it a revolt against Israel's existence.

The most ignorant or incoherent report on the summit was by CNN's Christiane Amanpour on October 16. Describing Palestinian protests against the meeting, she explained:

> They felt [Arafat] was strong-armed into coming here, that he would come here and come back with absolutely nothing. And they also felt that it was too close to the killings and the casualties. They thought there should be a decent interval before any kind of summit.

It was unclear how Amanpour derived her interpretation of Palestinian motivations, but her explanation defied logic. The demonstrators were demanding a continuation of the violence. How could they want that and also a "decent interval"? Obviously there could not be any interval until they stopped their violence. Moreover, the notion of a "decent interval" implied that violence was repugnant to them. That was why they were demanding more of it?

Once again, the most pro-Palestinian tilt was seen on ABC. On the first day of the summit, anticipating that Arafat might refuse to call for a halt to the intifada, Jennings leapt preemptively to his defense: "An Israeli government . . . cannot simply order its most extreme citizens to stop mistreating Palestinians. And while the Israelis say that Yasir Arafat can simply tell all the Palestinians what to do, the evidence suggests he cannot" (October 16). But the issue was not whether all Palestinians would obey an order from Arafat to end the violence; it was his conspicuous refusal to issue such an order. And the invocation of "extreme" Israelis "mistreating Palestinians" was gratuitous; it referenced no story. In fact, the Israeli government does endeavor to prevent its citizens from abusing Palestinians, although of course it does not always succeed.

Gillian Findlay's ensuing report echoed Jennings's theme:

> The Israelis insist Yasir Arafat could stop all of this. He could use his police to keep the stone throwers off the streets. He could shut down Palestinian radio and TV, which Israel says incites the crowds. And he could order his armed militia, the Tanzim, to never open fire, not even in self-defense. Yasir Arafat could give all of those orders, Palestinian leaders say, but it wouldn't make much difference.

This was yet another shot at the same straw man Jennings had already pummeled. How much difference an order from Arafat might make could be discovered

only if Arafat would give the order, but he would
not. And the formula about ordering his gunmen not
to fire "even in self-defense" was tendentious.
Although they were taking far more casualties, it
was the Palestinians who were initiating the violence, as their terminology acknowledged: they were
engaged in an "uprising."

Then, after a bit of an interview with Hanan
Ashrawi, Findlay continued: "Seven years of talking with Israel [have] produced nothing. Exactly
what extremist groups told Mr. Arafat would happen." The suggestion seemed to be that not only
was it understandable if Arafat did not compromise at Sharm al-Shaykh, it would be wrong for him
to do so, perhaps even to have gone there at all.
Findlay, it seemed, was endorsing Hamas's stand.

The next night, Findlay went on without any
noticeable shift: "The fundamental problem is that
the Palestinians on the street don't see that they
have any obligation to stop. The violence has all
been from the Israeli side, they insist. They
have a right to protest, and they will continue"
(October 17). With the summit consummated, Jennings
seemed to take the side of the Palestinian "protesters," complaining that the agreement announced
by Clinton was too pro-Israel: "Palestinians will
try to prevent violent demonstrations. Israel *may*
pull back its forces from some Palestinian territories if Israel believes the latest Palestinian
uprising has ended," his voice emphasizing the
word "may." This assertion did not merely violate
journalistic integrity; it was false. Israel had
committed, as was widely reported in other outlets, to pulling back its forces from the Palestinian population centers if the violence there
ceased for forty-eight hours.

On CNN, correspondent Rula Amin reported from
Gaza on demonstrations against the summit: "Once
again, the familiar pattern. The Palestinians throw
stones. The Israelis respond with tear gas, rubber-coated bullets, and live ammunition" (October
16). But this was false, or at least incomplete.

As had been widely reported, the familiar pattern
(probably followed by these demonstrations in Gaza,
as well) included not only stones from the Palestinians but also Molotov cocktails and gunfire.
Amin's report contained another important item
from which neither she nor other journalists drew
the obvious inference. "Almost every Palestinian
faction was present," she stated, "from the commu-
nists to Islamic fundamentalists . . . to Yasir
Arafat's supporters. All were united by the principle [that] their president must not compromise
on basic Palestinian demands." But if Arafat's
faction turned out for the demonstration, it could
only be because he wanted them to, suggesting
that the much-reported Palestinian pressure on
Arafat was a tactic in which he himself colluded.

Also that evening, CNN's Andrea Koppel came
up with a mystifying explanation for the weeks
of mayhem: "When Camp David ended without an
agreement, Palestinian despair eventually led
to violence" (October 16). This may have been
true, but as the normally evenhanded President
Clinton made clear, it was the Palestinians who
had refused to negotiate at Camp David. At the
very least, if Koppel's view was accurate, it
cried out for some explication about the rela-
tionship between the Palestinians and their
representatives.

Jennings was not the only one to take an
anti-Israel tilt during the week of the summit.
In the *New York Times* "Week in Review" section,
David Shipler, tracing the breakdown of the peace
process, wrote, "Trust was undermined when the
right-wing Israeli government [of] Netanyahu
built more Jewish settlements and dragged its
feet on carrying out commitments to relinquish
territory" (October 15). Trust, however, is a
two-way street, and Shipler was silent on the
violations of the peace process by the Palestinians, such as the failure to amend the Palestinian Charter to accept Israel's right to
exist, as promised, or Arafat's speeches to Arab

audiences suggesting that the accords were only a tactic for eventually gaining control of the territory of Israel as well.

In the *Washington Post,* Keith Richburg wrote, "Barak is already talking to his right-wing political opponents about forming a 'national emergency government.' . . . Israeli hard-liners . . . warned they will not look favorably on any outcome that seems likely to revive peace efforts" (October 16). In truth, the view of hardliners to whom Barak was talking about a unity government was not opposed to "peace efforts" but to what they saw as the overly generous terms that Barak's dovish government had offered. In a separate story that same day, Richburg wrote about Israeli military fire in Hebron that, as he reported, the Israeli military stated was aimed at Palestinian snipers. Yet, Richburg interviewed the owner of a bullet-riddled house that had been the Israeli target and reported credulously that he "said no one had ever shot at the Israelis from his house."

When Israel announced the arrest of a group of Ramallah residents whom it had identified as participants in the police station lynching, CBS's David Hawkins expressed alarm: "The arrests . . . almost certainly required the infiltration of Israeli commandos into Palestinian territory. That fact alone could rekindle Palestinian fury" (October 18).

More numerous than the examples of outright anti-Israel tilt in that week's coverage were reports that drew a false equivalence between the two sides. *New York Times* correspondent Jane Perlez wrote that "Mr. Sharon's provocative visit to Muslim holy sites . . . the destruction of . . . Joseph's tomb . . . and the burning of an ancient synagogue . . . have challenged the very notion of respect for and sovereignty over religious sites" (October 15). Surely Sharon's tour of the Temple Mount (which happens also to be the holiest site in Judaism and where he made no attempt to enter al-Aqsa mosque) bore no parallel to the

the destruction of the two Jewish holy sites.
Also in the *Times*, John Kifner, reporting on the
kidnapping in Europe of Israeli businessman
Elchanan Tannenbaum by Hizballah, added gratuitously at the end that "Israeli operations inside Lebanon are hardly unknown" (October 16).
After giving a few examples, he commented even
more gratuitously: "The Israelis were not always
infallible. A Moroccan waiter was killed in
Lillehammer, Norway." This was true, but the story
was decades old and had no relation to the snatch-
ing of Tannenbaum, nor was it analogous. It seemed
to have been appended to the story for no other
reason than to remind the reader that Israelis
have done bad things, too.

The *Post*'s Hockstader reported that "each leader
has made overtures to his most intransigent and
hawkish opponents. On the Palestinian side, Arafat
has reached out to Hamas. . . . And on the Israeli
side, Barak has invited Sharon to join his government" (October 15). The parallelism was mis-
placed, even ugly. Hamas had been explicit in its
aim of destroying Israel, a goal that it had
pursued by relentlessly trying to murder as many
Israelis as possible. Sharon, on the other hand,
although a hardliner, had said he was prepared to
make compromises to achieve peace, even if the
concessions he was prepared to offer were too
modest to interest the Palestinians. (He had, for
example, supported the forceful uprooting of Jewish
settlements in Sinai in order to fulfill the 1978
peace agreement with Egypt.)

Anticipating the summit, Keith Richburg wrote,
"Both Barak and . . . Arafat will . . . be riding
forces they may not fully control—populations
with hardened attitudes and less interest in making peace then in laying blame and extracting
revenge" (October 16). This may have been true
for the Palestinians, who were forever proclaiming days of rage and seemed committed to pros-
ecuting their "uprising" until victory. But Israelis
were in a state of despair as years of hope for

peace went down the drain. The formula of the peace process, "land for peace," acknowledged that peace was the Israeli desideratum. For the Palestinians, it was land. And now they seemed to believe that they had found a different path to that goal. Richburg's parallelism was unfair. The falseness of it was inadvertently highlighted in the illustration he offered:

> For Palestinians, the pertinent image going into the summit has been that of a 12-year-old boy, Mohammed Aldura, who was shot to death by Israeli soldiers while crying helplessly, cradled beneath his father's arm. For Israelis, the image has been the mutilated body of one of their soldiers being dumped from the window of a Palestinian police station in Ramallah and a young Palestinian gleefully holding out his hands to the screaming crowd below to display the soldier's blood.

As seen earlier, it is likely that al-Dura was not shot by Israelis at all, but even if he was, it was an accidental shooting in a crossfire initiated by the Palestinians. So distressed were the Israelis by the boy's death and so eager to make clear their regrets, they even accepted blame prematurely. In contrast, the Ramallah victims were set upon with clearly murderous intent by a lynch mob that joyfully celebrated the deed afterward.

On CNN, the day after the summit, correspondent Ben Wedeman reported that

> opposition to the Sharm al-Shaykh agreement remains strong on both sides. A coalition of Palestinian opposition groups, including Hamas, declared their determination to carry on the uprising. And Israeli opposition leader Ariel Sharon, accusing Israeli prime minister Ehud Barak of being soft on the Palestinians, has let it be known he will not join Prime Minister Barak in an emergency government.

The fault in the analogy here is that Sharon's refusal to join a coalition government in no way

impeded Israel's compliance with the agreements
that it had made at the summit, whereas the Palestinian groups could indeed make Palestinian
compliance difficult. But since Arafat did not
even try to comply, that was perhaps a moot point.

In a like vein, the network's Jerrold Kessel
reported on the south Jerusalem Israeli neigh-
borhood of Gilo, into which Palestinian gunmen
had been firing repeatedly from the town of Beit
Jalla, drawing Israeli return fire. The result,
stated Kessel, was "two communities united in
fear, hatred, and an appetite to punish the other"
(October 18). This was simply false. The Israelis
wanted to be left in peace, not to serve up
punishment. But what could they do except respond
to Palestinian fire?

episode 5:

The Election
of Sharon

The al-Aqsa intifada
spelled political doom
for Prime Minister Ehud
Barak. Already governing without a reliable majority in the Knesset, he had gambled that a
peace breakthrough with the Arabs would rally the
public behind him. But with the peace process
buried beneath the rubble of the new Palestinian
uprising, Barak was compelled to face elections
in early 2001. His principal opponent was Ariel
Sharon, who had won the standard of the Likud
Party to widespread surprise, as he had long been
presumed dead politically. The stain on Sharon
was a grievous one. As the mastermind of Israel's
1982 war against the Palestine Liberation Organization (PLO) in Lebanon, Sharon had arranged
with his Lebanese Christian allies for their mi-
litias to enter the Palestinian refugee camps of
Sabra and Shatilla to clean out PLO fighters
believed to have secretly remained behind in vio-
lation of an agreement for their exile. Instead,
the militia massacred many hundreds of civilians, and an official Israeli inquiry later held
Sharon "indirectly responsible" for this crime.

Nonetheless, with Barak's peace strategy having failed dramatically, and with the Israeli
public wishing for a government to take a strong
hand against Arab violence, the phoenix-like Sharon
defeated Barak by a wide margin. U.S. news coverage of this election might have been expected to
produce many instances of unfair treatment of
Sharon or of Israel for selecting him. Various
surveys have shown that journalists, especially
in the elite media, are disproportionately Democratic in their personal party allegiance, and
they might be expected to favor the Labor Party
over the Likud Party in Israel, even more so given
the strong themes of an alien nationalism at the
core of Likud ideology, not to mention the additional baggage carried by its standard-bearer.

Somewhat surprisingly, however, little of this
appeared in the news outlets reviewed for this

study. In covering Sharon's landslide victory,
there was less tendentious reportage treating Israel in a jaundiced light than during most other
moments of the intifada. It was as if the journalists, who had seemed so mesmerized by Palestinian
"rage," were sobered by Israeli anger at the Arabs, which had expressed itself at the ballot
box.

There were, of course, exceptions. *New York
Times* reporter Dexter Filkins referred to Sharon's
"reputation as one of the region's harshest men"
(February 7, 2001). Did Filkins not know that
Israel is located in the Middle East? The Ba'athist
elites of Iraq and Syria were bathed in blood.
The theocrats who ruled Iran were responsible for
the death and torture of untold numbers of their
citizens as well as for a global reign of terrorism. The Islamists of Algeria massacred hundreds
of thousands of their compatriots, many of them
women and children. Those of Egypt were not much
milder. The Sudanese regime prosecuted a devas-
tating civil war against the south of the country. There were also Osama bin Laden, Abu Nidal,
and countless other terrorist leaders whose lives
were consecrated to nihilistic bloodletting. Sla-
very, "honor" killings of nonvirgins, and various
other barbaric practices thrived throughout the
region. What were Filkins and his editors think-
ing?

In a February 4 *Times* article, Deborah Sontag
also offered a predisposed summary of Sharon's
conception of peace:

> An end to the conflict . . . in [Sharon's] view . . .
> would entail an evolution of the Palestinians
> and of the Arabs to the point where they whole-
> heartedly accepted Israel's existence and Israel's
> terms for existence.

The word "wholeheartedly" and the phrase "Israel's
terms for existence" were expressions of sarcasm
on the part of a hostile reporter rather than an
honest effort to capture Sharon's position. A

fair rendering of his position could have instead used the word "sincerely" and the phrase "entered into meaningful compromises to resolve the issues outstanding between the two sides."

When the election result was announced, *Times* correspondent Neil MacFarquhar reported that around the Arab world, "the most common response was a collective shrug about the defeat of Ehud Barak . . . , stemming from the sense that all Israeli leaders have treated Arabs with equal violence no matter what their party" (February 8). In reality, the Arabs have behaved more violently toward Israel than vice versa, most Israeli violence has been retaliatory, and Israel has relentlessly sued for peace. It may be true that the Arabs feel that it is they who have been the victims of violence, but this is a highly distorted, self-exculpating image. MacFarquhar, however, echoed this image in terms that appeared to lend it credence.

Most of the television networks carried stories that included much criticism of Sharon but nonetheless presented a clear and fair image of why Israeli voters chose him. For example, on the eve of the voting, NBC's Martin Fletcher, recalling Sharon's role in the Sabra and Shatilla massacres, noted ironically, "A government commission recommended he never be defense minister again. Instead, he could be elected prime minister" (February 4). At the same time, Fletcher conveyed the meaning of the election with a sound bite from a single voter who stated: "The center wants one thing: not to get killed."

Likewise, in the wake of the vote, Fox's Jennifer Griffin was hard on Sharon. "He promises to bring peace to Israel, but his critics say that all he knows is war," she stated, adding that his conception of peace "will put him on a collision course with the Palestinians, and it's hard to see how he will avoid more violence in the region" (February 6). But she also explained: "Israeli voters have said, in effect, that they are tired of feeling helpless in the face of Palestinian violence and that they hope Sharon will . . . return a sense of security and strength to the Jewish state."

CBS's David Hawkins, characteristically, was more jaundiced. On February 6, he spoke of Sharon's "hardline opposition to compromise with the Palestinians," which was a tendentious characterization. He might as easily, and more truthfully, have phrased it: "Sharon's unaccommodating terms for compromise with the Palestinians." And he explained the vote this way: "After five months of fighting and nearly 400 dead, most Israelis have given up on a negotiated peace. Today, they chose the general they believe is most capable of protecting Israel's security." This was partially accurate, although the assertion that Israelis had "given up on a negotiated peace" was wide of the mark. The true point was that Israelis had concluded that Arafat was not a sincere negotiating partner.

As usual, the most prejudiced report was to be found on ABC. Jennings led off the election-night coverage. "On *World News Tonight,* a new leader in Israel," he began. "The Arabs and many Israelis think he will lead the country into war. . . . There is no more divisive figure in Israel, and . . . the Palestinians hate Ariel Sharon" (February 6). Then, Gillian Findlay reported in with a series of commentaries on Sharon from his Israeli political opponents, which she did not bother to balance by presenting any of his supporters. Unlike the other networks, ABC gave its viewership no comprehensible explanation of why Israeli voters had chosen Sharon except perhaps that they were bloodthirsty.

NBC, Fox, and CNN all reported that the Palestinians had responded to Sharon's victory by proclaiming yet another "day of rage." According to the findings of this study, neither CBS nor ABC chose to report this.

episode 6:

The Gaza Incursion

In April 2001, for the first time, Palestinians fired mortars from the Gaza Strip into Israel proper. Israel had suffered rocket attacks across its border with Lebanon at many moments in its history, and these had led to major military actions. The prospect of a similar pattern developing along its southern border with an incipient Palestinian state was viewed with gravity. In response, Israel launched a military incursion into the strip, which it had ceded to the governance of the Palestinian Authority (PA) under the terms of the Oslo Accords. Although comments by Israeli military officers suggested that their plan was to remain in Gaza for an extended time, the Israeli force withdrew after one day, apparently bowing to the pressure of the United States after Secretary of State Colin Powell denounced the Israeli action as "excessive and disproportionate."

The Gaza incursion was reported in the *New York Times* by Jane Perlez, who quoted Powell's rebuke and went on to substantiate it implicitly: "The [Israeli] assault followed a fierce Israeli bombardment of Palestinian targets in Gaza, all in response to a Palestinian mortar attack" (April 18). There was something in Powell's words "excessive and disproportionate" that invited comment. Until that moment, the military doctrine for which Powell had been noted was the use of overwhelming force. "Cut it off and kill it," was how he had explained his strategy for handling the Iraqi army in the 1991 Gulf War. His criticism of Israel was thus a contradiction of what he had previously advocated. But the *Times* refrained from noting the contradiction. If President George W. Bush had, say, demanded that Japan increase its income tax rates, it is hard to imagine that *Times* reporters would have resisted the temptation to point out how this contradicted his own economic program.

Just two days before the Gaza incursion, Israel had responded to ongoing attacks from the

Lebanese group Hizballah by striking a Syrian radar station in Lebanon, since Israel held Syria—the dominant force inside Lebanon—responsible for encouraging Hizballah's activity. The Israeli strike was reported in the *Times* by Deborah Sontag, whose April 17 account of it was laced with opinion. "A deadly Israeli airstrike on a Syrian radar installation deep inside Lebanon unsettled the Arab world today just as Israel was receiving the first Arab official to visit since Prime Minister Ariel Sharon took office last month," she began. (The official was Foreign Minister Abdallah al-Khatib of Jordan.) Some paragraphs later, she added:

> Before the Israeli airstrike, something of a backlash had been building against Hezbollah inside Lebanon. . . . But the Israeli raid will most likely increase support for Hezbollah. The organization is seen across the Arab and Islamic worlds as the sole group actively doing something to counter Israeli violence.

This passage sounded a lot like the editorial that the *Times* ran the same day chastising Israel for the strike; it certainly was not reportage. And the last sentence was an Orwellian inversion; Hizballah's cachet was based on perpetrating violence, not countering it.

On April 16, *Washington Post* correspondent Daniel Williams reported the strike against Syria as "Sharon's second escalation within a week," although each was in fact a retaliation for an Arab attack. He also asserted that "peace talks between Israel and Syria brokered by the United States collapsed last year, after Israel declined to withdraw from the entire Golan Heights." This was an extremely biased version of the failure of the Israeli-Syrian negotiations and flatly false. Israel had indeed offered to withdraw from the entire Golan Heights; this was never in question. Yet, the negotiations foundered over where, on the narrow strip between the heights and the Sea of Galilee, the border would be drawn. Syria demanded to hold on to a small piece of land that it had seized on the banks of the lake in 1948. This territory was not part of the recognized international boundary. Syria had agreed to withdraw from it in its 1949 ceasefire agreement with Israel but did not fulfill the terms.

The same day's paper carried a separate article by Williams, a lengthy feature on Israeli settlements. "In contrast to the shifting U.S. stances, human rights groups have taken an unbending position that the settlements are illegal under the Geneva and 1907 Hague conventions," he wrote, quoting at length from a report by Human Rights Watch. No knowledgeable Israelis were quoted on the legal issues, although a strong argument can be made that Human Rights Watch was misapplying the law. Instead, Williams quoted one militant settlement leader as stating, "We don't consider this foreign land," an obviously unpersuasive reply since international law is not restricted to "foreign land."

The building of settlements in the West Bank and Gaza is probably Israel's most controversial policy, one that is unpopular even with many Israelis. There is nothing out of bounds in highlighting them in a feature story or in conveying the sharp criticisms. But there are also arguments to be made in defense of the settlements: that the land was captured in a war of self-defense against Arab aggression; that at Camp David Israel offered to withdraw most of the settlements; that if more than a million Arabs can live within Israel, Jews should be able to live within a future Palestinian state. Williams, however, chose not to convey any of these arguments to his readers. Instead, after quoting Human Rights Watch and several U.S. officials critical of the settlements as well as several West Bank Arabs with touching tales of being victimized by the settlement process or by the settlers, he "balanced" the report by quoting militant Israelis who put their case in a way sure to be off-putting. In addition to the weak point about international law, the

same militant stated: "No government can with-
stand the pressure [to build ever more settle-
ments], because inside each Jew, there is a small
settlement movement. It's the essence of Zionism."
To rebut other criticisms, Williams had another
Israeli say that settlements are "good for the
Arabs. They are employed building the settlements." In short, instead of making an honest
effort to achieve journalist balance, Williams
wove together sympathetic quotes from Arabs and
unsympathetic quotes from Israelis to make a tap-
estry whose every thread made Israel look bad.

The television coverage of these days of violence was marked by contrasts among the networks.
The evening news came on soon after the Israeli
attack on Gaza began but before it was clear that
Israel intended to occupy some ground. On ABC,
Peter Jennings began: "Israel is attacking Palestinian Gaza from land and sea and from the air. . . .
Earlier, Palestinians fired mortars into an Israeli town near the border" (April 16). CBS's Dan
Rather reported the same story in a different
tone: "Israeli helicopters and tanks fired on Palestinian targets in Gaza [to]day. The attacks
were in retaliation for Palestinians' shelling of
Israeli towns." Jennings's choice of words made
the Israeli action sound ominous, and his use of
the curious term "Palestinian Gaza" (is there some
other Gaza?) conveyed his own conviction that the
Israelis had no right to be there.

Jennings pursued this theme the next night as he
announced, "The Israelis invaded the independent
Palestinian territory of Gaza. . . . The Palestinians are furious, and the Bush administration says
it is excessive and disproportionate." Then, Gillian
Findlay came on to tell viewers again that "Palestinians are furious," adding that "Palestinians say
[Sharon] revealed his true intentions with this
attack." This last sentence sounded ominous, but
Findlay left it at that, explaining neither what it
was meant to imply nor why she had included it. On
CNN, Wolf Blitzer's take on the day's events sounded

a lot less alarming and was more enlightening
with regard to Israel's motives than Findlay's
reference to mysterious "true intentions." "As
quickly as it entered, the Israeli government
announced it was pulling out of the small corner
of Gaza it had reoccupied," stated Blitzer. Then
he added: "On Monday, Palestinians in Gaza lobbed
mortar shells into Israel. . . . It was seen by
Israel as a major escalation."

Jennings's inclusion of Powell's harsh description of Israel's action was entirely in order, but
the previous evening, as he and ABC correspondent
Hilary Brown reported the Israeli airstrike in
Lebanon, they conspicuously refrained from mentioning the U.S. position, even though the State
Department had made a strong statement that was
reported elsewhere. CBS, for example, in reporting the strikes, mentioned the Syrian and Israeli
positions and also that of the United States. It
showed State Department spokesman Richard Boucher
saying: "We condemn this escalation in the cycle
of violence that was initiated by Hizballah in a
clear provocation designed to escalate an already
tense situation" (April 16). But ABC viewers heard
only that "Israeli warplanes hit a Syrian radar
position" and that "[t]he Syrian foreign minister
said it was a flagrant aggression. Israel said
the strike was in retaliation for Saturday's attack on an Israeli border patrol by Hizballah"
(April 16). It seemed that ABC was faster to
include the U.S. government position when the
latter was critical of Israel than when it was
critical of Israel's enemies.

Some reporters at CBS might have fit in better
at ABC. Apparently to counterbalance Boucher's
interpretation that Hizballah was at fault and to
put the onus back on Israel, correspondent David
Hawkins added this comment: "Regardless of who
started it, Israel's air strikes have thrown cold
water on attempts to restart peace talks. They
also risk turning what's so far been a low-inten-
sity conflict with the Palestinians into a wider

war" (April 16). Hawkins's reportage was repeatedly harsh toward Israel, although others at CBS,
such as Rather, took a different tone. Such varia-
tion was typical at the networks, with the exception of ABC, where Jennings and his correspondents
were uniformly hard on Israel.

On NBC, the analogue to Hawkins was correspondent Andrea Mitchell. As Israel began its assault
on Gaza, she reported: "Israel launches a relent-
less attack on Gaza from the land, sea, and air—
for the first time, going back on an agreement,
seizing land it gave up seven years ago" (April
17). Not only was this characterization of the
incursion somewhat heavy (after all, this "re-
lentless attack" was over in one day), but the
part about "going back on an agreement" was false
and put blame on Israel unfairly. Nothing in the
Oslo process required Israel to foreswear self-
defense, nor did the PA hold sovereignty over the
territories it governed until a final-status agreement was achieved. In fact, it was the PA that
had gone back on the agreement, which explicitly
disallowed it to have mortars, much less to fire
them into Israel. For Israel to respond to such
an attack with military measures was well within
its rights under Oslo as well as customary international law.

The harshest broadcast of the week came from
CBS's Hawkins on April 19, an unusually long essay
putting all of the blame for the ongoing impasse
between Israel and the Palestinians on Sharon:

> During the Camp David peace talks last year, it
> was Yasir Arafat who turned down Ehud Barak's
> peace proposal, insisting on all or nothing. Now
> Israel's new prime minister, Ariel Sharon, is
> offering the Palestinians nothing at all. Sharon
> says he won't give back any more land, especially
> not in Jerusalem. He also rules out the removal
> of any Jewish settlements from the Palestinian
> territories.
>
> The Palestinians, Sharon says, must settle
> for less than half of the land in the West Bank
> and Gaza Strip, essentially what they have now.

And since coming to power, the former general
has dramatically ratcheted up Israel's military
response to terrorist attacks. He's launched air
strikes on Syrian positions in Lebanon and invaded Palestinian territory handed back in previous peace deals, drawing sharp criticism even
from the United States. Sharon's hardline policy,
offering no compromises, is intended to wear
down Palestinian resistance against Israeli occupation of Palestinian territory. It's all stick
and no carrot.

That means more fighting and bleak prospects
for peace. Even if Yasir Arafat called an end to
the intifada, it's doubtful that he could stop it
completely. And Israel refuses to negotiate until all Palestinian violence ends.

It's usually the Palestinians who are criticized for not being serious about making peace
with the Israelis. Now that notion is being challenged by an Israeli government that seems un-
willing to compromise.

episode 7:

The Dolphinarium

The first of the inti-
fada's massively deadly
suicide bombings occurred
on June 1, 2001, outside the Dolphinarium, a Tel
Aviv disco. It claimed twenty lives, mostly teen-
age girls. Yasir Arafat at first responded with a
vague statement opposing violence in general, but
German foreign minister Joschka Fischer, who happened to be visiting Israel and the Palestinian
Authority at the time, insisted on a clearer denunciation of the crime. Fischer himself helped com-
pose such a statement, and Arafat put his name to it.

New York Times correspondent Deborah Sontag
reported that "for the first time since . . .
violence began eight months ago, Yasser Arafat
made a public call . . . for an immediate and
unconditional cease-fire" (June 3). This sentence
may have driven home just how doggedly Arafat had
resisted making any such appeal until that moment, something that had rarely been made clear
in news reports that devoted many column inches
and minutes of airtime to claims that Arafat was
incapable of stopping the violence. Sontag's article also quoted an Israeli official likening
Arafat to a "zookeeper who opens all the cages of
the lions and tigers," referring to his release
from custody early in the intifada of known terrorists and bombmakers. But Sontag found the analogy
lacking in political correctness, so she hastened
to add that this was "a comparison that many Palestinians would find objectionable."

Summarizing the intifada just before the bombing, *Washington Post* correspondent Lee Hockstader
repeated yet again, as if it were fact, his debat-
able belief that the "Palestinians rose up against
continued Israeli occupation in the West Bank and
Gaza Strip" (May 30). He went on to write that "most
Western governments and human rights organizations
regard the Jewish settlements as illegal under
international law. Israel insists that international law does not pertain to the West Bank and
Gaza." Hockstader offered no quote or other evi-

dence for this last sentence, and it was false, a
dishonest way of making Israel's position look un-
supportable. Israel's true position was not that
international law did not apply but rather that
Israel's critics' interpretation of the law was
erroneous.

A week or two before the Dolphinarium murders,
Prime Minister Ariel Sharon had announced a "policy
of restraint" in the hope that the recently released Mitchell Commission report might prove to
be the impetus for an end to the months of violence. U.S. diplomats had called on the Palestinians to reciprocate. Hockstader, however,
insinuated that the Israeli policy was fraudu-
lent, writing, "In recent days, as Israeli forces
observed what [Assistant Secretary of State Wil-
liam] Burns called the policy of restraint, Israeli bulldozers and tanks entered Palestinian
territory and uprooted fields and orchards, Palestinians say" (May 30). There was no way for a
reader to know whether this was true and, if so,
what the reason might have been. Yet, the day
after the Dolphinarium attack, Hockstader reported
that the attack had intensified the "pressure on
Prime Minister Sharon to renew airstrikes, assas-
sinations and other attacks . . . which had been
suspended under a policy of restraint for the
last two weeks. . . . On Thursday [the day before
the bombing] Sharon encountered a bitter outpour-
ing of criticism for his policy of restraint"
(June 2). Apparently, the restraint was not so
illusory after all.

The Dolphinarium attack, with so many young,
innocent victims, and coming as it did while Israel was pursuing a policy of restraint, created
a moment of sympathy for Israel. Furthermore, to
the astonishment of many Israelis and most of the
outside world, Sharon opted to continue his policy
of restraint, and he refrained from retaliating.
The result was that very little in the press
reports on this occasion exhibited the unfriend-
liness toward Israel that was evident on many
other occasions during the al-Aqsa intifada.

episode 8:

The *Karine-A*

On January 4, 2002, the
Israeli government an-
nounced that its forces
had intercepted a ship, the *Karine-A,* on the high
seas laden with arms bound for the Palestinian
Authority (PA). This amounted to a serious viola-
tion of the Oslo Accords. The principal reassur-
ance that Israel had sought in ceding territory
and acquiescing in the prospective establishment
of a Palestinian state was that this state would
not become a threat to Israel. Two days after the
announcement, the Israeli government invited reporters to a show-and-tell session at which all
of the arms were laid out on display. These arms
made an impressive haul, but a question remained
about to whom they belonged.

In the *New York Times,* correspondents James
Bennet and Joel Greenberg reported that "Palestinian officials denied any link to the ship," and
that U.S. officials "said they had no evidence the
weapons were destined for the Palestinian Authority, and instead raised the possibility that the
arms were headed to . . . Hezbollah" (January 5).
The authors quoted the PA minister of information, Yasir Abed Rabbo, who affirmed, "We insist
that the Palestinian Authority has nothing to do
with this ship." Similarly, in the *Washington Post,*
Hanna Rosin reported that Yasir Arafat "denied
having any knowledge of or involvement with the
ship, and his information minister [Abed Rabbo]
said the announcement of the raid was 'a theatri-
cal game'" (January 5).

The next day, the *Times'* Greenberg reported
once again that "Palestinian officials have vehemently denied any links to the shipment" (January
6). And the following day, the *Post*'s Rosin reported that "Palestinian officials continued to
deny any involvement with the ship . . . and
accused the Israeli government of fabricating
charges." She quoted the Palestinian minister of
international cooperation, Nabil Sha'ath, who
stated, "In time, these allegations will prove to

79

be unfounded." And she added an excerpt from a statement issued by the PA that said it was "not involved in this incident and such steps are not part of its policies and it can not be involved in any such operations of this sort at a time it is fighting to end violence."

On January 8, however, the two newspapers carried reports that resolved the question about the ownership and destination of the shipment. The *Post*'s Associated Press story ran as follows:

> The Palestinian naval captain captured by Israeli commandos with 50 tons of weapons on his ship said today that he was a member of Palestinian leader Yasser Arafat's Fatah movement and that the arms were intended for the Palestinian-controlled Gaza Strip. 'I'm a soldier. I obeyed orders,' said the captain, Omar Akawi, in a prison interview. He added that he picked up the rockets, mortars and antitank missiles in the Persian Gulf, off the Iranian coast. Akawi, who was captured Thursday along with 12 crewmen in the Red Sea, said he worked in the Palestinian Transportation Ministry and received his instructions from an official in the Palestinian Authority.

Despite confirming that Akawi was "a mid-ranking member of [the PA's] naval unit," the story proceeded:

> The Palestinian leadership . . . continued to insist that the Palestinian Authority had nothing to do with the weapons shipment. 'It's a kind of propaganda, unfortunately,' said Ahmed Qureia, the Palestinian parliament speaker. 'It's a false way to undermine the peace process.' . . . Arafat reiterated today that he knew nothing about the shipment.

That same day, the *Times* ran a similar report by Bennet based on an interview with Akawi, who, it said,

> identified himself as a 25-year member of Mr. Arafat's Fatah organization and a naval adviser to the Palestinian Authority's transport minis-

try. . . . [He] said he knew that he was shipping
munitions but not the precise contents of his
cargo, which arrived packed in submersible can-
isters. . . . '[T]hey told me it was weapons for
Palestine, and I am a Palestinian officer merely
doing what he has to,' he said. 'It is my people's
right to defend itself.'

In what was perhaps the most damaging statement
in Bennet's report because of the duplicity that
it underlined, the captain revealed that "he had
expected to receive orders canceling his mission
after Dec. 16, when Mr. Arafat gave a speech
calling a halt to military operations. . . . No
such order came." In the same article, Bennet
also reported what seemed to be a tactical shift
in Arafat's response: "Mr. Arafat told Javier
Solana, the European Union's foreign policy chief,
that any Palestinian found to be involved in the
smuggling would be punished. He said he would
welcome international help for a Palestinian investigation of the Israeli accusations."

On the networks, CBS and CNN carried the story
of the ship's capture the day it was announced. On
CBS, David Hawkins stated:

Palestinian officials say they don't know anything about the arms shipment. One called the
seizure an Israeli propaganda stunt, timed to
sabotage U.S. special envoy Anthony Zinni's attempt to restart peace talks. They say it's the
Israeli government that's not serious about returning to the negotiating table, pointing to
continued Israeli raids into Palestinian territory. . . . Both Palestinians and Israelis say
they want a ceasefire that will stick. The problem is both sides think the other side's lying.

On CNN, Mike Hanna showed Arafat advisor Nabil
Abu Rudeineh stating, "We know nothing about this
ship which the Israelis are talking about. . . .
We consider it an Israeli propaganda in order to
sabotage the mission of General Zinni." And then
Hanna concluded: "Both sides remain as suspicious
of the other's pledges of peace as ever."

Despite having reported these denials, neither network's evening news chose to revisit the subject during subsequent days to inform viewers that the evidence of PA sponsorship of the shipment had become quite clear. One might have thought that the titillation of the mystery about the ship would have augmented its news value—which was in itself considerable because of the geopolitical implications—and that the combination would have easily justified the airtime. One would have thought, too, that the case for reporting the solution to the puzzle was strengthened for these two networks by the fact that both Hawkins and Hanna were at least to some extent taken in, as shown by Hawkins when he stated "both sides think the other is lying," and Hanna with his similar words. As it turned out, it was the Palestinians who were lying, they knew they were lying, and therefore they also knew that the Israelis were *not* lying. Hawkins, in short, was dead wrong. Hanna's formulation was broader, but it too was off. Given the ship incident, the Israelis had an ironclad reason for being "suspicious of the other's pledges of peace." But the Palestinians had no such obvious reason for suspicion of the Israelis, and therefore a probing reporter might have wondered whether the Palestinians' claims to this effect were genuine or were a method of covering their own duplicity.

On January 11, however, CBS anchor John Roberts did report that

> Yasir Arafat's Palestinian Authority announced it has detained two senior Palestinian officials and is seeking another on suspicion of trying to smuggle arms into Gaza. Last week, Israel's navy stopped and seized a Palestinian-owned ship which was carrying fifty tons of weapons and ammunition. The Israeli government blamed Arafat, who denies the charge.[9]

This, at least, informed viewers that the link to the PA had been proved, although the report was credulously agnostic about Arafat's role. Given that the whole gamut of Palestinian spokesmen had vehemently denied any connection with the ship, this sudden, dramatic shift to the claim that Palestinian officials were involved but that Arafat had no idea might have invited some journalistic skepticism. CBS exhibited none.

On NBC, the story was first reported not on the day the ship was captured, but two days later, at the news conference at which Israel presented the captured arms. Correspondent Martin Fletcher described a "war chest of weapons bought, says Israel, by Yasir Arafat, breaking interim peace accords that limit what weapons and how many Arafat can have" (January 6). This crucial bit of explanation of the diplomatic implications was absent from the other networks' reports. NBC then showed a clip from Palestinian minister for Jerusalem affairs Ziad Abu Ziad, who stated, "We are not involved. We don't have money to buy such weapons, and war is not on our agenda."

Like CBS, NBC did report the PA's announced arrest of two of its own for their involvement with the ship, allegedly behind Arafat's back. But in contrast to CBS's credulous account, NBC's January 12 report also included an interview with the head of Israeli army operations, who insisted that Arafat was behind it all. (And, indeed, he was. It was the proof of this, furnished by Israel to Washington, together with Arafat's denials, that eventually led the U.S. administration to turn its back on Arafat as a peace partner.)

Fox, which did not report the story on its evening news until the day the ship's captain was made available to the press, put it clearly. Correspondent Jennifer Griffin stated, "Palestinian officials have denied knowledge of the shipment, but in an interview . . . the ship's captain confirmed the weapons were destined for the Palestinians" (January 7).

ABC broadcast the story on the evening the Israelis showed off the cargo. After clips of Israeli officials blaming the PA, correspondent

Hilary Brown reported that the "Israelis' claims
are hotly denied by the Palestinian Authority"
and showed Information Minister Abed Rabbo stating, "We are sure the Authority has nothing to do
with such allegations" (January 6). Brown then
added, "State Department officials say they have
no evidence of Israel's claim and are withholding
judgement on the case." Although this made ABC's
account seem the most skeptical among the networks of Israel's charges, ABC did not return to
the story any time over the next ten days to
report Akawi's revelations or other evidence that
eventually proved those charges to be true.[10]

episode 9:

The Powell Mission

Following a suicide bombing in Netanya during Passover that proved to be the deadliest attack to date, Israel launched "Operation Defensive Shield," its largest military operation of the intifada, on March 29, 2002. For the first time since it had yielded the urban centers of the West Bank to the Palestinian Authority, Israel reoccupied these territories, aiming to arrest or kill terrorists and to destroy their weapons and bombmaking facilities. On April 11, while these operations were under way, Secretary of State Colin Powell arrived in Israel for a high-profile attempt at personal mediation of the conflict. After six days Powell left, able to report little progress. Press coverage of Israel's offensive reached a crescendo over the military operation in Jenin, where several blocks of buildings were flattened and where Palestinians claimed that Israeli forces had committed a massacre.[11]

U.S. officials and many other observers were surprised at Yasir Arafat's refusal to make the gestures Powell sought toward bringing the violence to a halt. *New York Times* correspondent David Sanger explained Arafat's intransigence by shifting the blame onto Ariel Sharon. "Palestinians are so humiliated and enraged at their treatment by Mr. Sharon that no call from the United States [for an end to terrorism] makes much impression," he wrote on April 13, although this analysis conspicuously failed to explain why similar U.S. appeals before Sharon was in office had had no effect. Sanger's colleague Serge Schmemann also grasped for explanations that would make Arafat's behavior understandable. "Palestinians have been irritated by what they perceive as a double standard from Washington, with pressures on the Palestinians to condemn suicide bombings, but no condemnation of the heavy casualties inflicted by the Israeli Army on Palestinian civilians, which the Palestinians refer to as 'state

terrorism,'" he wrote on April 14, as if anyone
who genuinely wanted peace might be deterred by
such irritation.

Also during Powell's visit, Israel announced
that it had captured Marwan Barghouti, chief of
the al-Aqsa Martyrs Brigades, a new wing of Arafat's
Fatah movement that had been increasingly involved in suicide bombings and other attacks against
Israelis. *Times* correspondent James Bennet wor-
ried that "the arrest . . . complicat[es] . . .
Powell's effort to arrange a truce" (April 16). He
reported, "Palestinians insist that Mr. Barghouti
is a politician, not a military man," something
that could be said as well about all of the heads
of terrorist groups. Members of the group, Bennet
added credulously, "have said they respect Mr.
Barghouti . . . but do not act on [his] orders in
conducting attacks," as if they would tell Bennet
on whose orders they do act. Bennet closed out his
report with a quote from a Palestinian legislator
who alleged that Barghouti's Israeli captors "will
torture him in a very, very bad way. They want him
to say that Arafat supports Al Aksa Brigades."

The *Washington Post* did not stretch so to put
Arafat in a good light, but its correspondent
Alan Sipress reached just as far to read malig-
nity into Sharon's actions. Reporting on the side
trip that Powell made to meet with Lebanese and
Syrian officials, Sipress added this bit of interpretation: "Sharon, unmoved by U.S. demands
that he immediately end his West Bank invasion
and reluctant to address Palestinian political
demands, has sought to turn Powell's attention to
other matters" (April 16).

It may have been that Sharon urged Powell to
speak to the Lebanese and Syrians, as Israel has
often asked U.S. officials to do. But the problem
on the Israel-Lebanon border was all too real,
and U.S. concern was genuine. Continuing attacks
and threats from Hizballah threatened to create a
"second front" that could even grow into a full-
scale Arab-Israeli war since it would bring Is-

rael into confrontation with Syria. It is unlikely that any prodding from Israel was required
to persuade Powell to try to calm these troubled
waters. But even if Israel did encourage Powell
to address this issue, Sipress's suggestion that
it did so out of ulterior motives—namely, to
deflect attention from the Palestinians—was either tendentious or uninformed. Far from being
some sort of pretext, the Lebanese frontier has
long been one of Israel's most urgent security
concerns.

Surprisingly, the networks devoted a larger
portion of their stories to Powell's mission than
the newspapers did, perhaps because their news
focus more closely tracks the activities of U.S.
government leaders. On ABC, correspondent Gillian
Findlay reported that "as he prepares to
leave . . . , [Powell] doesn't have what he came
for: from . . . Sharon, a timeline for a troop
withdrawal. Without that, Palestinians say there
is little chance Yasir Arafat will renounce violence" (April 16). This put the onus on Israel,
but it was a dishonest formulation. Findlay had
been covering the intifada from day one, and she
must have known that there was little chance that
Arafat would renounce violence whether or not he
received a timeline for the end of the Israeli
operation. Or, at least, there was little chance
that he would make an earnest effort to carry out
any such renunciation.

Only days before, Arafat himself had provided an inadvertent reminder of just how unre-
liable any such declaration from him would be.
Powell's arrival had been marred by yet another
suicide bombing; this one, which killed six and
wounded nearly a hundred in a Jerusalem market,
was carried out by a female belonging to Arafat's
own al-Aqsa Martyrs Brigades. In response, Powell
called off a scheduled meeting with Arafat until the latter denounced the action. Accord-
ingly, Arafat issued a statement saying, "Our
steady principle . . . rejects using violence

and terror against civilians. . . . We declared this position beginning in 1988" (Associated Press, *New York Times,* April 14). Were fourteen years not enough time for ABC to catch up with this game?

CBS, in contrast, demonstrated appropriate skepticism. On April 13, Wyatt Andrews reported:

> It sounded just like Arafat proclamations of before, this condemnation of violence. But there on Palestinian TV came a statement in Arafat's name, condemning all terrorist activities that target civilians, whether Israelis or Palestinians, especially the last one that occurred in Jerusalem.

After adding that "Arafat's response passed the Powell test" for rescheduling their meeting, Andrews went on to ask and answer the obvious question: "Why would the secretary accept the condemnation of a bombing from the man widely believed to have sent the bomber? Because Powell is on a peace mission, and he wants a shot at telling Arafat to his face, 'It's time to deliver.'"

The next evening, after Powell's meeting with Arafat, Andrews reported:

> There was no commitment from Arafat to stop. Arafat's chief negotiator, Saeb Erekat, said Palestinians want to end the violence but that Israel's West Bank incursion must end first. 'Once the Israelis complete their full withdrawal,' Erekat says, 'we will then carry out our obligations.'

A few weeks later, Israel did withdraw its forces from Palestinian cities (although keeping them on the outskirts). This, however, was not followed by any reduction in violence by Palestinians.

The most remarkable report on CBS was by chief White House correspondent John Roberts on April 17, who showed a clip of President George W. Bush saying that "a murderer is not a martyr . . . just a murderer," and then explained why he found this declaration regrettable. According to Roberts,

Bush's "admonishment reinforced a growing belief in the Arab countries and beyond that the president's Mideast policy is rooted too heavily in domestic support for Israel and ignores the suffering of the Palestinian people." This was thinly veiled code for a denunciation of the "Jewish lobby," frequently expressed abroad but rarely in the United States.

That same evening, Andrews seemed to have forgotten his earlier skepticism toward Arafat, and now pointed a finger at Israel as the offending party:

> Prime Minister Sharon, [Powell] said, finally set a weekend deadline to end the West Bank invasion, but the fact that troops are still there now, Powell admitted, killed any chance of achieving a ceasefire. . . . For a week now, the Israelis have said they are withdrawing, but some tanks leave and then return. Israel explains it's just searching for individual suspects, but across whole villages around East Jerusalem, new curfews have been imposed.

On NBC, Andrea Mitchell reported that Powell "called upon Israel . . . to stop using excessive force" (April 13). But this terminology was not Powell's. The Arabs were accusing Israel of excessive force, which Israel denied. Powell had diplomatically avoided pronouncing judgment on the issue, artfully calling on Israel to "refrain from the excessive use of force" without saying whether it already had been guilty of this. Mitchell's subtle paraphrase changed the meaning of Powell's remark and served to smuggle a little editorial into her news report. At the conclusion of Powell's visit, she reported that "U.S. officials say Powell pushed Arafat hard on terrorism and security. But no progress on a ceasefire was possible because Israel has still not pulled back" (April 17). Although Mitchell was consistently harsher toward Israel than her colleagues at NBC were, in this instance it appears that her slant, like Wyatt Andrews's turnabout on CBS, reflected briefings

by a Powell entourage that was upset with Sharon
and perhaps with Bush, too. Mitchell hinted at
this as she added, "Tonight, Sharon has more le-
verage than ever over U.S. policy, a frustrating
lesson for Powell."

CNN, too, expressed skepticism toward Arafat's
statement against terrorism. "It was really . . . very
strong language . . . that Yasir Arafat used," reported Andrea Koppel on April 13, too generously,
since in truth this language was boilerplate. But
she added: "He has condemned acts of terrorism
before, but what he has yet to do, say U.S. and
Israeli officials, is to translate those words
into concrete action."

The next evening, CNN correspondent Jerrold
Kessel reported that "Sharon has called Colin
Powell's decision [to meet with Arafat] a tragic
mistake, fearing it might serve to rehabilitate
the Palestinian leader as a peace partner." This
was a distorted presentation of Sharon's fears. He
had made quite clear his conviction that Arafat
could not be a peace partner because Arafat did
not really want peace. Sharon did not fear a peace
partner; he feared the resurrection of a cloak of
respectability for a man whom he saw, with good
reason, as a terrorist uninterested in peace. To
this, Kessel, who had never in the dispatches
reviewed for this study bothered to criticize
inconsistencies or hypocrisies in Arafat's positions, pointed to one he espied on the part of
Israel's leader. Sharon, he said, "has abandoned
his long insistence that there should be no negotiating under fire. Now he's the one who's press-
ing for negotiating a ceasefire under fire, under
his fire." Apparently, Kessel thought he had made
a clever observation, but it was too clever; Sharon
was not after a ceasefire. Even if he were, Kessel's
point made no sense. Ceasefires are only reached
when there is fire—otherwise, what is to be
ceased?

The arrest of Barghouti elicited this sympathetic portrait from ABC's Peter Jennings on April

15: "He was in favor of the peace process until, as he told an Israeli newspaper, the Israelis didn't withdraw from the territories and went on building Jewish settlements." Gillian Findlay chimed in admiringly that "Marwan Barghouti never hid his beliefs." For CBS's David Hawkins, the arrest of Barghouti provided a lens on Israel's deeper nefarious objectives. "Palestinians insist he's a politician," said Hawkins before interviewing Palestinian leader Sari Nusseibeh, who said, "Marwan is actually—[has] always been . . . an extremely positive force in the peace process" (April 16). Neither interviewer nor interviewee attempted to explain how it could be, then, that Barghouti was credibly charged with masterminding terrorist actions that had killed dozens of Israeli civilians or that he was known to be the head of the al-Aqsa Martyrs Brigades, whose very name—"Martyrs"—trumpeted its role in suicide-murder missions. Hawkins rounded out the report with a bit of strident editorializing: "Almost all Palestinians, and even some Israelis, don't believe this is a war just against terrorism. They see it as a war to destroy the Palestinian Authority and prospects for a Palestinian state." This vicious interpretation of Israeli motives ignored the simple fact that the war was the Palestinians' initiative and that Israel had desperately sought an end to the violence. If the Palestinians stopped attacking Israelis, was there any reason to believe that Israel's military action would continue?

During these days, there was much in the *New York Times* about the violence on the ground. On April 13, United Nations (UN) correspondent Barbara Crossette reported, "The secretary-general said the United Nations, with about 12,000 relief workers in the Palestinian camps and settlements, had been getting reports that Israelis had violated the codes of conduct in war." She gave readers no way to know that the fifty-plus-year-old UN relief operation in the Palestinian camps was

far from an independent or objective source. It
had become instead an integral part of the Palestinian polity, and the vast majority of those
12,000 relief workers were themselves Palestinians. Similarly, the *Times* ran a Reuters story on
April 15 asserting that "the European Union [is]
losing patience with Israel's West Bank offensive," a formulation that obscured the fact that
the European Union had staked out a strongly anti-
Israel position since the outbreak of the violence and indeed before.

Several other *Times* stories implied criticism
of Israel. Serge Schmemann reported that the Israeli offensive had caused "enormous destruction"
(April 13). "Editorial Observer" Steven Weisman
stated that "Mr. Sharon's drive against the Palestinians has turned out to be more brutal than
expected" (April 13). And on April 14, the paper
carried Associated Press reports citing Arafat's
claims of massacres in Jenin, Ramallah, Nablus,
and Tulkarm. Yet, the April 14 issue of the *Times*
also ran an illuminating account by Michael Gordon
of the nature of the war Israel was fighting,
providing context that, except for NBC, was offered
in none of the other media reviewed for this study:

> For Israeli forces, it is also an especially
> dangerous mission. This is not an American-style
> military campaign that uses airstrikes for weeks
> or even months before ground troops are deployed.
> It is urban warfare, with soldiers moving [from]
> alley to alley, house to house, searching for
> militants amid booby-trapped homes. Twenty-four
> Israeli soldiers have been killed and 124 wounded
> since the operation began on March 28.

Operation Defensive Shield occasioned a remarkable *Times* editorial that seemed to reflect the
underlying assumption of much of the news coverage. It opined that "real Israeli security will
prove elusive until the occupation of the West
Bank ends and Palestinians are permitted to . . .
establish their state" (April 15). Because this
study is concerned primarily with the accuracy

and fairness of reportage, comments on editorials or columns appear only in a few places. Yet,
this *Times* editorial embodied such a fanciful
leap of faith that it warrants mention. Had the
Times merely asserted that Israel would continue to suffer trouble from the Palestinians
as long as it occupied the territories captured
in 1967, the argument would have been hard to
gainsay. But the editorial went further. It
suggested that the evacuation of the territories and the creation of a Palestinian state
would lead to "real security" for Israel. There
was not a shred of evidence for believing this.
On the contrary, all relevant experience cast
it into doubt, beginning with the fact that
Israel had never enjoyed security before 1967
and that the current violence had been unleashed
in the face of Israel's offer of a Palestinian
state containing almost all the territory in
question. The *Times* is of course entitled to
its editorial opinions, but it is disturbing
that such an influential organ should propound
beliefs as unreasonable as these.

Although coverage of the allegations of a massacre in Jenin peaked after Powell's visit (and
will be the focus of "episode 10" of this study),
there were many stories about Jenin that coincided with the visit. On April 13, a nonbylined
item on casualty statistics in the *Times* stated
that "Israel has officially said 100 Palestinians
died in Jenin, but some Israeli officials have
put the actual toll nearer 200. Palestinians put
the Jenin figure at several hundred." And *Washington Post* correspondents Keith Richburg and Alan
Sipress reported, "Palestinians have said that
Israeli troops killed hundreds . . . mostly civilians, in . . . Jenin," adding that "Palestinians compared the killing in Jenin to the deaths
of Palestinian refugees at . . . Sabra and Shatilla"
(April 13). The next day, Richburg and Sipress
repeated these figures as well as the Sabra-Shatilla
analogy.

On April 15, however, the *Times*' Serge Schmemann
and Joel Greenberg reported a change in numbers:
"Once the bulldozers moved in and resistance waned,
the [Israeli] army spoke of 100 to 200 Palestinian deaths. But after the ensuing furor, the army
today said it was aware of 45 Palestinian dead."
The reference to the "ensuing furor" seemed intended to cast doubt on the new figures, and the
two authors went on to claim that it was the
original, higher Israeli figures "that prompted
Palestinian charges of a massacre." This attribu-
tion was far-fetched. Arafat, after all, was also
crying massacre in Nablus, Ramallah, and Tulkarm,
where no such Israeli figures had been put out,
and indeed he had been denouncing Israeli "massacres" repeatedly since the first days of the
intifada. In the *Post,* Sipress and Richburg now
reported that the Israeli army said it had discovered thirty-nine bodies "after searching about
half the camp" (April 15).

On ABC, correspondent Dean Reynolds reported
on April 14, "Today, at the Israeli cabinet meeting, ministers referred to dozens of dead Palestinians from the fighting in . . . Jenin—considerably
below the hundreds to which they referred only
days ago." Visiting Jenin, evidently with an Israeli military escort, Reynolds reported that "on
the tour, a Palestinian doctor was encouraged [by
the Israelis] to offer details which seem to have
been rehearsed with soldiers beforehand." Reynolds's
sensitive journalistic antennae apparently alerted
him to the possibility of getting a doctored story
of events. Not once, however, in the period reviewed for this study did anyone at ABC exhibit a
similar alertness to the possibility of manipulation by the Palestinians.

On CNN, Wolf Blitzer reported on April 13, "We
have new pictures of the devastation in the Jenin
refugee camp. . . . Palestinians allege a massacre. Israel says there were hundreds killed or
wounded." That same evening, correspondent Sheila
MacVicar stated, "The Israeli military is now ac-

knowledging . . . that at least 100 people died"
in Jenin. Then, Blitzer interviewed Nasser al-
Kidwa, the Palestinian representative to the UN,
who charged

> obvious war crimes which have been committed . . .
> the horrible war crime in the refugee camp in
> Jenin. . . . This was willful killing. This was
> wanton destruction. This was massacres . . . war
> crimes under international law . . . this is
> unheard of.

Two nights later, Blitzer interviewed Sharon,
who denied that a massacre had occurred at Jenin
and said that Israel now believed that the number
of Palestinian dead counted in the dozens. This
was followed by an interview with Palestinian
minister of international cooperation Nabil
Sha'ath, who insisted that the massacre story was
genuine. "We don't know the exact number, because
already a lot of the bodies have been snatched
and buried elsewhere in unidentified graves that
we learned about," he said. "[Sharon] took six
days to perpetrate the massacre and six days for
a cover-up" (April 15).

The debate about Jenin dragged on, as "episode
10" of this study will show. In the end, the
Israeli figures would be vindicated by a UN investigation, while every version put out by the
Palestinians would turn out to have been hope-
lessly erroneous and propagandistic.[12]

episode 10:

The Jenin
'Massacre'

Although Israel's military action in Jenin was mostly ended by April 11, it was not until a few days later that Israel allowed journalists into the area. This may have lent some credibility to claims that a massacre had occurred there, and the reportage of the claims and denials reached a crescendo about a week after the events had taken place.

The first *New York Times* story filed from Jenin was by David Rohde, who reported that "in interviews, [residents] accused Israeli forces of shooting civilians, removing bodies and bulldozing houses with people inside" (April 16). One resident

> led a group of reporters to a pile of rubble where he said he watched from his bedroom window as Israeli soldiers buried 10 bodies. 'There was a hole here where they buried bodies,' he said. 'And then they collapsed a house on top of it.'

Rohde acknowledged that the "Palestinian accounts could not be verified," but he seemed to give them the benefit of the doubt: "The smell of decomposing bodies hung over at least six heaps of rubble today, and weeks of excavation may be needed before an accurate death toll can be made."

On April 17, Rohde ran a long story on the complaints of aid organizations that Israel was not giving them sufficient assistance, quoting one unnamed worker as saying "the devastation is worse than I expected. . . . I couldn't have imagined anything worse than this." On April 18, the paper carried Rohde's account of Palestinians digging body parts out of the rubble, seemingly buttressing the massacre claims.

In the early stages of the fighting, Israel lost thirteen soldiers in a single event set off by a booby trap. After that, Israel changed tactics, and instead of entering buildings in pursuit of enemy fighters, used armored bulldozers to knock down buildings from which Israeli forces had been fired upon. On April 18, Rohde reported:

> Israeli officials say they issued clear and re-
> peated warnings over megaphones to residents to
> leave the camp, particularly in areas where houses
> were bulldozed. But Ms. Daoud, who is blind and
> partly deaf, said she had never heard any Is-
> raeli orders to leave the camp, or the bulldoz-
> ers flattening houses nearby.

Was the reader supposed to infer that Israel's claims of having given warning were not true?

One of the factors tilting press coverage of Jenin to Israel's disadvantage was the highly vis-ible and agitated role of Terje Roed-Larsen. A Norwegian diplomat working for the United Nations (UN), Roed-Larsen had been a driving force behind the Oslo Accords and perhaps was distraught at seeing his project come to such a bad ending. *Times* correspondent James Bennet quoted Roed-Larsen as stating, "Combating terrorism does not give a blank check to kill civilians" (April 19). This, like most of what Roed-Larsen had to say during this period, was extremely wide of the mark. The subsequent UN report noted that approximately fifty-two Palestinians in all died in Jenin.[13] By Israel's count, thirty-eight were gunmen and four-teen civilians.[14] Human Rights Watch, known for being highly critical of Israel, estimated that twenty-two of the fifty-two were civilians.[15] That is fewer than the twenty-three Israeli soldiers who died in Jenin. These numbers clearly bespeak a military operation at pains to avoid civilian casualties, the opposite of the picture that Roed-Larsen was eager to paint.

When President George W. Bush applauded Israel's withdrawal from Jenin, *Times* correspondent David Sanger objected: "On a day when Arab, European and United Nations officials were focused on the de-struction that the Israeli incursions had left behind, . . . Mr. Bush's comments may bolster Pal-estinian suspicions that the United States was supporting Prime Minister Ariel Sharon" (April 19).

The reports from Jenin came amid a tense standoff in Bethlehem, where scores of Palestinian gunmen had taken refuge in the Church of the Nativity. *Times* correspondent Serge Schmemann reported, "The Israelis had begun detaining some wives and mothers of men inside, Palestinians said" (April 17). Some women may have been detained, perhaps with due cause, but it seems very unlikely that any systematic activity of the kind described by Schmemann took place because no other news organizations reported it—nor did the *Times,* according to the findings of this study, repeat this claim.

Washington Post correspondent Molly Moore painted a vivid picture of the destruction in Jenin. At the same time, however, she got on top of the massacre story days before the *Times* or the networks lent any similar illumination. On April 16, she reported: "Interviews with residents inside the camp and international aid workers who were allowed here for the first time today indicated that no evidence has surfaced to support allegations by Palestinian groups and aid organizations of large-scale massacres or executions by Israeli troops. Thus far, about forty bodies have been recovered." But three days later, the *Post*'s John Lancaster was resurrecting the massacre tale with the help of Roed-Larsen and some other international participants. "What we are seeing here is horrifying," said Roed-Larsen, "horrifying scenes of human suffering. . . . Israel has lost all moral ground in this conflict" (April 19). Lancaster also quoted Human Rights Watch official Peter Bouckert, who stated, "I think it's clear that in the end what actually happened in Jenin will fall somewhere in between what the Palestinians are alleging and what the [Israeli Army] claims. But only an independent authority can establish what actually happened."

When the UN conducted its investigation, however, what was "clear" to Bouckert proved incorrect. Far from splitting the difference, the UN's conclusions coincided more or less exactly with Israel's claims and not at all with those of the Palestinians. Lancaster returned to the subject the next day, writing that "Palestinian officials said many civilians died in the Israeli assault on Jenin" (April 20).

On ABC, Peter Jennings introduced a report on April 17 by Gillian Findlay that he clearly believed—or wanted viewers to believe—constituted a kind of "gotcha" moment, proving the worst of Israeli intentions. It was based on Palestinian claims that Israeli soldiers had torn up the Palestinian Ministry of Education in Ramallah. Jennings began the segment with these words:

> If you have listened with even half an ear to the verbal conflict between the Israelis and Palestinians, you will have heard Israelis say repeatedly that whatever they did, it was to root out terrorism. Whereas, the Palestinians have said that Prime Minister Sharon is trying to undermine Palestinian society.

Then he introduced Findlay, who reported:

> Amid all the damage—smashed buildings, torn-up roads, power and water systems that no longer work—there has been another casualty here: the Palestinian Authority itself. This is the Ministry of Education: doors blown in, offices trashed, employees who say they were forced at gunpoint to lead soldiers from room to room. . . . The soldiers, [one employee] says, then went for the computers—ripping our hard drives, confiscating financial records, student records. He says they even blasted the ministry's vault, taking canceled checks and $10,000 in cash.

She then brought on Saeb Erekat, who claimed that "everything of the civilian infrastructure and security infrastructure have been destroyed," before finally giving an Israeli spokesman time for a single cursory sentence in defense of his government's actions. This was the merest bow to balance in a report whose unmistakable import was made clear by Jennings's lead. But did it really prove what Jennings wanted viewers to believe it did?

Israel may indeed have ransacked the ministry's offices, although the specifics provided by ABC were all from Palestinian sources, leaving reason to doubt such details as the theft of cash. But did this show, as Jennings implied, that terrorism was not Israel's true target, that Israel was only using terrorism as an excuse in a war whose true goal was to stamp out Palestinian national aspirations? Only if one believes that the same Palestinian Authority that sponsored terrorism even while nominally rejecting it, and that repeatedly closed schools in order to send children into the front lines, would be above using its Ministry of Education as a front for terror-related activities. Perhaps Jennings believed this, but his implied accusation of Israeli duplicity meant that Israel, too, must believe Arafat would never misuse his Ministry of Education in this way. And this Israel assuredly did not believe.

Given Jennings's ill-concealed animus toward Israel, Roed-Larsen's fulminations fell upon him like manna from heaven. He began his April 18 broadcast by quoting Roed-Larsen's words that the scene in Jenin was "horrifying, beyond belief." During that week, a new ABC reportorial voice, that of John Yang, was added to the coverage of the conflict, and he was clearly singing from the same page as his colleagues. On April 19, three days after the *Post*'s Molly Moore had reported on the absence of evidence of a massacre in Jenin, Yang reported from that city: "There is no firm estimate of how many Palestinians died here. The Israeli armies [*sic*] say it's in the dozens. The Palestinians say it's in the hundreds, maybe the thousands." And the next evening, Yang was declaiming, "All this destruction here in Jenin is becoming a rallying cry for the Arab world. A symbol of Israel's iron-fist approach."

By any reasonable standard, the low number of civilian casualties as compared with the number of Israeli casualties proved just the opposite. An "iron-

fist approach," such as armies—including Arab armies—
confronting terrorism have often taken in other
places, would have led to civilian casualties many
times higher. For example, when militants in the
Syrian town of Hama challenged the rule of dictator
Hafez al-Asad in 1982, Asad's forces leveled much
of the town, causing an estimated 20,000 deaths—
nearly 1,000 for every civilian that Human Rights
Watch said had died in Jenin. *That* was an iron-fist
approach.

On CBS, anchor Dan Rather exhibited none of
the bias of ABC's Jennings, but he, too, chose to
quote Roed-Larsen. Unlike Jennings, however, he
included Israel's version as well: "Israel says
its troops did their best to minimize civilian casualties. . . . But . . . one United Nations official
calls Jenin, quote, 'a sad and disgraceful chapter in
Israel's history'" (April 18). On April 19, CBS correspondent Mark Phillips used a story about Israel's
withdrawal from Jenin to deliver himself of a
long editorial accusing Israel of destroying the
prospects for peace:

> Moderates on both sides here feel trapped in a
> cycle of violence. . . . Nobody's expecting the
> recent relative lull in violence to last. What
> has this Israeli operation accomplished? . . .
> It has only reduced, not destroyed, the Pales-
> tinian capacity for revenge, and it certainly
> hasn't reduced their motivation. Among the casu-
> alties . . . have been the voices of moderation
> and compromise.

Phillips had apparently been assigned to the region just that week, and he sounded as if he were
entirely unaware of what had transpired during
the preceding year and a half. Such platitudinous
moral equivalence had been blown to smithereens
by the suicide bombers. It was Arafat and his
Fatah group who were supposedly the Palestinian
moderates, but they had morphed into the al-Aqsa
Martyrs Brigades, which was running neck-and-
neck with Hamas and Palestinian Islamic Jihad in
its efforts to murder Israeli civilians. And on

the Israeli side, where indeed there were plenty of genuine moderates, the violence they felt "trapped in" was Palestinian violence.

On April 20, Phillips pounded away at his *idée fixe* of moral equivalence. "What happened in Jenin depends on who you believe," he said, citing the contrasting Palestinian and Israeli versions. "Even the UN inquiry . . . isn't likely to end the argument over Jenin. In the bitterness and mistrust of this conflict, each side has basically already made up its mind over what happened there and who is to blame." Of course, in reality, what happened depended not on whom the observer believed. Whatever the state of mind of the two parties, there was an objective reality to these events, and journalists, one would have thought, were under a professional obligation to discover what it was, as best they could, as, for example, did the *Post*'s Molly Moore. But not Phillips, who sounded like a modern-day literary critic approaching a "text" of which all constructions were equally subjective, thus equally valid.

NBC's report from Jenin served to illustrate how poor the ABC and CBS coverage was. NBC was no less vivid in portraying the destruction that the Palestinians had suffered, but in a few brief passages it allowed viewers to see the Israeli side, too. It is ironic that a reporter like CBS's Phillips could strain so for artificial symmetry in order to present a surface balance yet fail in a substantive way to tell both sides of the story. On NBC, Tom Brokaw led by saying that Jenin had witnessed "some of the most intense fighting of the war," which had "leveled many homes and killed an undetermined number of Palestinians. On the Arab side, they're claiming it was a massacre. On the Israeli side, they're claiming that is an exaggeration" (April 16). Then correspondent Martin Fletcher reported from the scene:

> It's a rough ride into Jenin, but it's worse when you get there. The center of the refugee camp looks like it was hit by an earthquake, but it

was the Israeli army. Palestinians claim there was a massacre here, that close to 500 Palestinians were killed and their bodies taken by Israel and hidden in mass graves.

This gave a pretty clear view of the Arab take on these events, but Fletcher next showed an Israeli officer who said of the massacre allegation, "it's a complete lie." Fletcher went on to summarize the Israeli assessment of the numbers who died in Jenin. At this point his interview with the Israeli was interrupted by a couple of local women who came along and said, as Fletcher translated their words from Arabic: "We don't have food or water. . . . And where are our children? Maybe they're dead. Come with us. . . . You'll find dead bodies." This was pretty strong, seemingly spontaneous testimony for the Palestinian version. Fletcher, however, continued, pointing around him:

> But the problem here isn't only death but destruction. The Palestinians laid booby traps everywhere. These white cables were strung all over the camp. They were controlling booby-trap bombs, and here's one of the bombs. To protect their soldiers, the army brought in giant armored bulldozers to simply demolish booby-trapped homes. So, now the question no one can answer yet is: How many more bodies are buried under the rubble?

One could scarcely call this account pro-Israeli, but both sides of the story came across.

On CNN, Sheila MacVicar also provided a balanced account. She did not fail to dramatize the anguish of Palestinian deaths, closing her April 16 report with these words:

> How many bodies, how many fighters, how many civilians? No one yet knows. No one even knows how many might be missing. Only a few hundred of the camp's surviving inhabitants are still in their own homes. The rest are scattered and have not yet been counted. It is mostly women and children who are left. Some of them wandered the

camp weeping, crying for lost brothers and sons.
And they point to that mountain of rubble and
say that is where they lie.

Yet, MacVicar also included the Israeli perspective: "The Israeli military say this was the scene
of some of the fiercest fighting, and not a neigh-
borhood, they say, but a fortress . . . the heart
of the Palestinian terror infrastructure, and
the civilians who lived here, the women and children, they say, were used as shields." She also
put an Israeli on camera for a moment pointing
out some of the booby traps.

The next evening, Wolf Blitzer interviewed Saeb
Erekat, who claimed, "We have 1,600 missing men in
this refugee camp [in Jenin]" (April 17). Erekat
also called for "an international commission of
inquiry to get the results and to decide how many
people were massacred. And we say the number will
not be less than 500."

On April 19, when Israeli forces withdrew from
Jenin, Christiane Amanpour delivered a long report
from Jenin that had none of the balance that MacVicar
had shown. She spoke of Israeli forces "attacking
houses with Apache helicopters and tanks"; of residents who "say they never got any warning"; and of
Israeli soldiers "us[ing] Palestinian camp residents as human shields as they went house to house
searching for armed militants and booby traps,
[which] violates the rules of war." Although her
report included more details on the battle than
most other television news reports, she managed
not to mention the use of booby traps by the Palestinians (beyond the confused reference to Israeli
soldiers "searching" for them). It was the killing
of thirteen Israeli soldiers by booby trap that had
reshaped Israel's tactics in Jenin, but no viewer
would have learned this from Amanpour's account.
Instead, as she told it, Israel had resorted to
razing buildings because of the effectiveness of
Palestinian "armed resistance."

Also during this week, anchor Wolf Blitzer
conducted an interview with Ismael Abu Shanab,

one of the founders of Hamas, and asked him whether
Hamas would "accept an independent Jewish state
in this part of the world" if "Israel were to
withdraw completely to the 1967 lines" (April 16).
Shanab shot back: "We accept Israeli withdrawal.
And we said it many times, that we support Israeli
withdrawal to 1967." The evasion could scarcely
have been clearer, but rather than press Shanab,
Blitzer ended the interview and then summarized:
"He seemed to say that Hamas would support a Jewish state in Israel if Israel were to withdraw to
the '67 lines." Shanab had said no such thing;
accepting Israel's withdrawal is far different
from accepting Israel's existence. Blitzer, a former
reporter for the *Jerusalem Post,* is not unfriendly
to Israel nor ignorant of its security concerns.
Nonetheless, he seemed to whitewash Shanab's answer. Perhaps he could not bring himself to accept that Hamas's undisguised goal is the utter
destruction of Israel. But various polls demon-
strate that this is precisely what a great many
Palestinians and other Arabs say they desire.
Unless this brutal fact is absorbed, much else
that transpires in the painful struggles between
Israel and its neighbors will be seen through a
clouded lens.

conclusion

In the preceding pages, I have documented dozens of instances of inaccurate, tendentious, misleading, or unfair items found in the news reports that I examined. So what? To err is human, and journalists trying to cover a bitter, entangled conflict unfolding on many fronts—much of it in secret—are not likely to achieve perfection. And, too, the circumstances in which they work are often dangerous; for that they deserve our gratitude.

There are, however, some faults which ought not to be excused. The most serious of these is bias. By this I do not mean the biases that reporters, like everyone else, may hold within. I prefaced this study by specifying my own bias. Rather, I mean the betrayal of journalistic standards that occurs when reporters allow their biases to color their reportage, when what they purport to be news stories are in fact subtle editorials.

Of the news organizations I examined, the one whose bias was abundantly evident was ABC television, which in almost every episode under study made Israel look worse than it appeared in the reportage of the other networks or the two major newspapers. Invariably, this bias began with the comments of Peter Jennings, who, for example, wanted his viewers to believe that Israel was not really at war against terrorism but rather only using terrorism as an excuse for strangling Palestinian aspirations. Perhaps because Jennings takes a direct hand in writing the news reports and also in selecting many of the reporters (he has the title of "editor"),[16] ABC's reportage evinced a consistency of slant that I found in none of the other news organizations. During the period under review, viewers of ABC never saw, for example, as did those of other networks, the Temple Mount rioters showering stones and bottles on Jewish worshipers at the Wailing Wall below nor the booby traps in Jenin that impelled Israel to smash buildings. They would have learned, falsely, that Jewish settlers proclaimed "days of rage," when in fact it was only Palestinians who did so. They would have heard Palestinian spokesmen denying any involvement in the *Karine-A* arms shipment but would have seen no follow-up story of the proof of Palestinian involvement. And they would have heard many other claims from Palestinian sources without challenge, indeed often reinforced by Jennings and his reporters, such as that Yasir Arafat was completely helpless to stop the violence.

Other news organizations had individuals whose consistent anti-Israel slant stood out, for example, David Hawkins at CBS, Mike Hanna and Jerrold Kessel at CNN, Andrea Mitchell at NBC, Deborah Sontag at the *New York Times,* and Daniel Williams at the *Washington Post.* But unlike at ABC, these voices were balanced by others whose approach was less tendentious.

The best reportage was by NBC's Martin Fletcher. Fletcher was hardly soft on Israel. His coverage, for example, of the destruction of parts of Jenin was as vivid as that of any other journalist, but unlike most others, Fletcher presented a clear vision of the booby traps laid by Palestinian fighters so that his viewers could grasp what Israeli soldiers were facing.

What is the cause of bias against Israel? Perhaps some individuals are endemically hostile to the Jewish state, but such a deep cause is unlikely. A better explanation can be found in an essay by a correspondent for the *Economist* who described the Israeli-Palestinian conflict as "an epic struggle of the weak against the strong."[17] Since journalists often pride themselves on afflicting the powerful, those who see the Middle East in these terms would naturally find themselves siding with the Palestinians.

After bias, the next most serious journalistic failing is ignorance. Most journalists are necessarily generalists, so they cannot fairly be expected to be experts on each area they cover. Yet,

they owe it to their audience to be reasonably
well informed, to give themselves a crash course
upon being assigned to a new place. The one who
most conspicuously failed to meet this standard
was Christiane Amanpour, who plunged into Israel
apparently not even understanding such elementary
facts as that the settlers are Israelis who live
in the territories occupied in 1967 as opposed to
within Israel proper (which is why they are called
"settlers"); not knowing that Ehud Barak repre-
sented the dovish side of the Israeli spectrum;
and apparently believing that Hamas is opposed to
violence.

Beyond the failures of individual journalists or news organizations, I discovered one
systemic problem in the course of this study
that is probably more important than any one
individual's bias. These journalists seem to fol-
low a canon that says when two sides are fighting, it is their obligation to report equally
and with equal credence what is said by each.
But the quality of the information provided by
the two sides in this conflict is highly asym-
metrical. By this I mean simply that the Palestinians repeatedly lie. It starts with Arafat
and goes down to his many deputies. It seems
even to reach to doctors in Palestinian hospi-
tals and to many subjects of apparently unstaged
man-in-the-street interviews, such as the Jenin
resident who claimed to have watched Israel bury
ten bodies under a building.

Palestinian spokesmen asserted vociferously that
they had nothing to do with the *Karine-A*. They
insisted that 500 people had been "massacred" in
Jenin. Amid these claims, Israeli aerial surveil-
lance captured, and released to the press, photos
of a staged Palestinian funeral in which the "corpse"
could be seen running to the litter and climbing
into it.[18] Arafat also claimed that "massacres"
had occurred repeatedly in every Palestinian population center. Palestinian first lady Suha Arafat
declared in a speech in Ramallah, with Hillary

Clinton present as her guest, that Israel was
poisoning Palestinian wells. When Israeli forces
found a photo of a two-year-old Palestinian boy
decked out as a suicide bomber, Palestinian officials claimed it to be a fabrication until the
child's family acknowledged the photo. Arafat
claimed to have renounced terror while secretly
encouraging it. He declared his intent to conduct
a "very serious investigation" of the Ramallah
police station lynching of the two Israeli reservists, although nothing of the sort ensued.
Nor was the Jericho synagogue that was torched by
a Palestinian mob restored, as Palestinian spokesmen had claimed. A Palestinian died in an auto
accident, and his body was shown to journalists
as a victim of Israeli torture. (It was also shown
repeatedly on Palestinian television to encourage
rage.) And so on.

On the other side, Israel, while engaging in
public relations with all the spin and self-in-
terest that any democratic government is guilty
of, nonetheless operates, like other democratic
governments, with a presumption of truth-telling.
At least twice during these episodes, Israeli
spokesmen helped to reinforce stories embarrassing to their own side because that was what the
facts, at first glance, seemed to suggest. Only
later did Israel discover that these stories were
probably false or exaggerated. The first case was
the death of Mohammed al-Dura on the third day of
the intifada. Eventually, Israel's investigation
concluded that the boy had probably died from
Palestinian fire, and the research of German television network ARD reached a similar conclusion.
But at the time, Israeli spokesmen, eager to put
on record their regrets over the tragedy, accepted that Israeli fire had caused his death.
The second case was Jenin. At first, Israeli sources
said that as many as 200 Palestinians had died,
thus fueling the claims of a massacre. Only later
did Israel realize that the actual number was in
the fifties.

What happens in a conflict where one side, accustomed to operating with a controlled press, will say anything that seems to serve its purposes, without any conscience about its truth value, while the other side attempts to learn and tell the truth, at least to the degree of other democratic governments? Faced with this situation, have the media no obligation beyond reporting "he says, she says"?

The asymmetry of veracity is compounded by other asymmetries. For one, Israel, being a democracy, is rich in critics of its own government. Many of the leads to stories that make Israel look bad originate in the Israeli press, with Israeli nongovernmental organizations, or with representatives of the political opposition. There is no shortage of Israeli academics and intellectuals willing to be quoted or to go on camera criticizing their government's policies toward the Palestinians. There is, on the other hand, no comparable freedom in the Palestinian press. And the willingness of individual Palestinian notables to speak out against their government is sharply circumscribed. About a year and a half into the intifada, voices began to be raised among the Palestinians criticizing corruption and Arafat's style of governance, but only later were a precious few willing to challenge Palestinian violence against Israel. (On the other hand, calls by Hamas, Palestinian Islamic Jihad, and others for greater violence are widely aired and treated with respect.) In many stories I examined for this study, an assertion critical of some Israeli policy, for example, on settlements, would be prefaced with the phrase "even many Israelis believe . . ." And this was undoubtedly accurate. But I never saw, mutatis mutandis, a criticism of Palestinian policy with the phrase "even many Palestinians . . ."

Another important asymmetry is that the Palestinians have created a menacing environment for journalists. The Israeli daily *Ha'aretz* reported in October 2002 that when three Hamas members were killed in Gaza by an explosion, apparently of their own bomb, "A group of journalists who arrived at the scene of the blast, including an AP reporter and a photographer and a cameraman for Associated Press Television News, were assaulted by several Hamas supporters."[19] On August 26, 2002, the Associated Press reported, "The Palestinian journalists union declared . . . that news photographers are 'absolutely forbidden' from taking pictures of Palestinian children carrying weapons or taking part in activities by militant groups, saying that the pictures harm the Palestinian cause." In October 2000, London's *Daily Telegraph* carried an account by a British news photographer who came upon the aftermath of the Ramallah lynching:

> I reached for my camera. I was composing the picture when I was punched in the face by a Palestinian. Another Palestinian pointed right at me shouting 'no picture, no picture!' while another guy hit me in the face and said 'give me your film!' I tried to get the film out but they were all grabbing me and one guy just pulled the camera off me and smashed it to the floor. I knew I had lost the chance to take the photograph that would have made me famous and I had lost my favourite lens that I'd used all over the world, but I didn't care. I was scared for my life.[20]

Indeed, the whole grisly story from Ramallah might not have gotten out were it not for a single Italian film crew that managed to escape with footage of the killing. Ricardo Christiano, the bureau chief of the Italian television network RAI, was so frightened when he learned that the film was being attributed to his company that he wrote a letter, published in the Palestinian press, swearing that it was "not the official Italian television station RAI [that] filmed the events" but another station.[21] He pledged that "we always respect . . . the journalistic procedures with the Palestinian Authority for . . . work within

Palestine."[22] When this letter appeared, it set
off a ruckus in Italy that led to the recall of
Christiano. His friends later were quoted as explaining in his defense that of all the European
journalists who had received beatings at the hands
of the Palestinians, he had been beaten the most
severely, leaving him traumatized.

Nor should it be assumed that such violence
arises spontaneously from the grass roots rather
than being orchestrated by Palestinian officials.
When the Palestinian Authority was embarrassed in
its relations with the United States by demonstrations of jubilation over the terrorist attacks of September 11, 2001, *USA Today* reported
that "Palestinian Cabinet Secretary Ahmed Abdel
Rahman . . . called international news agencies
and said the safety of their staff could not be
guaranteed unless they withdrew the embarrassing
footage of Palestinian police firing joyfully in
the air."[23]

Just as there is no indication that news organizations have thought through how to handle the
imbalance in truthfulness between the two sides
in the conflict, so there is also no evidence that
they have weighed the implications of the intimidation aimed at both journalists reporting from
the Palestinian areas and Palestinians themselves
to discourage dissident opinions. In these re-
spects, the journalistic environment of the Israeli-Palestinian conflict is not a level playing
field.

A similar point was made by the *Washington
Post*'s editorial page editor, Fred Hiatt, regard-
ing the U.S. conflict with Saddam Husayn's regime
in Iraq:

> Because our default position is to tell the truth—
> might as well, unless there's some good reason
> not to—we have trouble imagining people for
> whom that is not so, for whom even a whispered
> conversation far from officials or listening de-
> vices can never be considered safe. . . . And we
> assume, because of our blessed poverty of imagi-

nation, that their officials behave more or less
as ours do, maybe lying when pressed, or when
they think they can get away with it, but telling the truth when, all things being equal, there
seems no reason not to.[24]

The conflict between Israel and the Palestinian
Authority is often described as a conflict between two peoples. And so it is, in part. But it
is also a conflict between an open, democratic
society and an authoritarian one in which violence and coercion are endemic. Whereas democratic governments practice public relations or
"spin control," authoritarian governments often
aim for something more, namely news management or
manipulation, which they try to achieve through
deceit and intimidation. Treating their domestic
news media as servants of the regime, they are
little inclined to respect the functions or objectivity of the foreign press.

Reporters tend to be savvy and tough; they are
not easy people to con or bully. Nonetheless,
authoritarian regimes have often succeeded in
twisting coverage to their purposes. Joseph Stalin
famously beguiled the *New York Times* into covering up, and even directly denying, the monstrous
famine that claimed five to ten million Ukrainian
lives in the 1930s. Adolf Hitler lulled the *Times*
of London into a benign interpretation of his
intentions, for which it issued a poignant mea
culpa after World War Two. And during his guer-
rilla days, Fidel Castro got the *New York Times*
and other news organizations to portray him as
nothing but a radical democrat, only to acknowl-
edge once he achieved power that he had been a
communist all along.

The various U.S. news organizations, as well
as the American Society of Newspaper Editors and
the Society of Professional Journalists, have codes
of standards and ethics that guide reporters in
dealing with their sources. But none that I have
found include instructions for handling the machi-
nations of authoritarian regimes, much less for

trying to balance the competing presentations of
democratic and authoritarian adversaries. In the
case of the Middle East, that lacuna seems to work
to Israel's disadvantage. Yet, it is not for Israel's
sake so much as for the sake of their readers and
viewers and the effectiveness of their profession
that journalists ought to give systematic consid-
eration to the problem of dealing with warring
parties that are so dissimilar in how they deal
with the press.

Endnotes

1. Jeffrey Goldberg, "Arafat's Gift," *New Yorker,* January 29, 2001, p. 55.

2. Quoted in "First Statement of the Government of Israel" submitted to the Sharm El-Sheikh Fact-Finding Committee (a.k.a. the Mitchell Committee), December 28, 2000, paragraph 183. Available online (www.mfa.gov.il/mfa/go.asp?MFAH0jcb0).

3. Yasir Abed Rabbo, "We Are Not Sending Our Children Out to Die," Palestine Liberation Organization, Negotiation Affairs Department, November 26, 2000. Available online (www.nad-plo.org/eye/opeds9.html).

4. "Drei Kugeln und ein totes kind" (Three bullets and a dead boy), originally produced as a documentary by local television station Hessischer Rundfunk, then broadcast by ARD on March 17, 2002, as an episode of the regular investigative series *Das rote Quadrat* (The red square). See also From Sommer, Allison Kaplan, and Herb Keinon, "German TV Report. Palestinians Likely Killed Gaza Boy," *Jerusalem Post,* March 20, 2002.

5. Michael Getler, "Tense *Times,*" *Washington Post,* June 9, 2002.

6. See note 4.

7. Ron Kampeas, "Ultimatum Looms for Palestinian," Associated Press Online, October 8, 2000; Barry Schweid, "Albright: Arafat Can Stop Violence," Associated Press Online, October 8, 2000.

8. "IDF: PA Planning Mosque at Joseph's Tomb," *Ha'aretz,* October 11, 2000; Margot Dudkevitch, "Palestinians Refurbish Joseph's Tomb," *Jerusalem Post,* October 11, 2000.

9. In keeping with the general method of this study in examining five-day segments, the dates that I have encompassed for this episode are January 4 through 9. Yet, in considering whether the networks followed through to show the solution to

the mystery embodied in the original story, it would have made no sense to cut off my inquiry arbitrarily on January 9, so I looked at the week beyond as well.

10. This was as far as I searched. It is extremely unlikely that the network returned to the story beyond this point, since it had already grown cold.

11. I have chosen to examine Powell's mission and the battles of Jenin as two separate episodes, even though the five main days of coverage of Powell's diplomacy overlap slightly with the five main days of coverage of Jenin, meaning that coverage of Powell was intermingled with news of the fighting. In keeping with my practice throughout this study of including whatever news stories about the Israeli-Palestinian conflict ran during the days of each selected episode, this episode, which focuses on Powell's mission, includes much material that also concerns Operation Defensive Shield and Jenin. Jenin itself is the focus of "episode 10" of this study.

12. The investigation concluded: "Fifty-two Palestinian deaths had been confirmed by the hospital in Jenin. . . . A senior Palestinian Authority official alleged in mid-April that some 500 were killed, a figure that has not been substantiated in the light of the evidence that has emerged." "Report of the Secretary-General prepared pursuant to General Assembly resolution ES-10/10," United Nations General Assembly, July 30, 2002, paragraph 56. Available online (www.un.org/peace/jenin).

13. Ibid.

14. Ibid., paragraph 57.

15. Ibid.

16. Gillian Cosgrove, "Brain Drain of Local Journos: Why U.S. Networks Have a Yen for Our Ink-Stained Wretches," *National Post* (Toronto edition), August 17, 2002.

17. Max Rodenbeck, "Broadcasting the War," *New York Times*, April 17, 2002.

18. See Israel Defense Forces Spokesperson's Unit, "Main Points of Briefing Given by Colonel Miri Eizen," May 2, 2002; available online (www.idf.il/english/news/funeral.stm). "Israeli Drone Films Palestinians Faking Funeral in Jenin," *Israel Insider* (Tel Aviv), May 5, 2002; available online (www.israelinsider.com/channels/diplomacy/ articles/dip_0204.htm). Independent Media Review Analysis, "Palestinian Group Admits Jenin Funeral Staged—But Claims Was for a Movie," May 5, 2002; available online (www.imra.org.il/story.php3?id =11834). Independent Media Review Analysis, "LAW Refutes Israeli Claims of Staged Jenin 'Burials,'" May 8, 2002; available online (www.imra.org.il/ story.php3?id=11896).

19. "Witnesses: Blasts at Militant's Gaza Home Kills Three," *Ha'aretz,* October 31, 2002.

20. Mark Seager, "I'll Have Nightmares for the Rest of My Life," *Sunday Telegraph,* October 15, 2000.

21. See Sharon Waxman, "On the Journalistic Front, Loaded Images," *Washington Post,* October 19, 2000.

22. Israeli Ministry of Foreign Affairs, "Coverage of the October 12 Lynch in Ramallah by Italian TV Station," press release, October 18, 2000. Available online (www.mfa.gov.il/mfa/ go.asp?MFAH0i2p0).

23. Matthew Kalman, "Palestinian Leaders Try to Repair Image," *USA Today,* September 13, 2001.

24. Fred Hiatt, "Lies in the Absence of Liberty," *Washington Post,* April 14, 2003.

048483